TAPESTRY
of LIFE

TAPESTRY
of LIFE

A quirky perspective of a cherished life

ANN SMITH

WATERCOLOR ILLUSTRATIONS BY SAVANNA SMITH

XULON PRESS

Xulon Press
2301 Lucien Way #415
Maitland, FL 32751
407.339.4217
www.xulonpress.com

Paperback ISBN-13: 978-1-6628-2707-5
Ebook ISBN-13: 978-1-6628-2708-2

Dedication

I lovingly dedicate this book to my daughter, Savanna, who was the unwitting inspiration for its creation, and for encouraging me through its fruition. She is my rock when I need one, as well as my motivation throughout life. Thank you, Munchkin. I love you!

Table of Contents

Acknowledgments

There are many people featured in this book; many of these are people who experienced with me those events that made a difference in my life, and who influenced me, each in their own capacity. Certainly, to those people I owe my gratitude and thanks.

For those of you who do not see your name in this book, realize I focused primarily on my earlier and more formative years; this does not mean that you have had no influence on this book. On the contrary, there are many people around me who encouraged me to finish the book, and then to pursue its publication; Savanna, Paula, and Ally, to name a few. Your encouragement was vital to help me bring to completion that which I had begun.

And Savanna, I wish to thank you for your active participation in this book by honoring me with your beautiful watercolor illustrations; please know how greatly they enhanced the final product.

Preface

When my mother unexpectedly passed away, I realized there were many 'blanks' I had left from her life. I knew her as a mom, and that was all. Not that that was bad, or that I was disappointed, but after she was gone, I discovered there were so many other facets to her life that I never knew. So many things that made her 'Marilyn', but I knew her only as 'mom'.

Many strangers, to me, stopped by the house in obvious shock and dismay to offer their personal and heartfelt condolences to us, so broken up they were over her sudden departure. One man came to the house and introduced himself to me as 'the guy she would wave to when she rode past on her bike', and he wanted us to know how much he would miss those waves. People whose lives she touched, and in whose lives she mattered and made a difference, yet I will never know how they fit into her puzzle.

There are things now I wish I would have asked, or that I could have known about her, experiences unique to her. But we were too busy living in the moment to really 'talk'. And maybe all daughters feel that way when they lose their mom. I do not know; I have never lost one before. I only know how I feel, and it is profound.

Not a day goes by that I do not wish I could have one more second with her, or another chance to say goodbye. Although I know she is with me in my heart for now and for always, this book, in some unconventional way, allows me to feel closer to her, even if just in memory.

And so, I created this book for my daughter, Savanna, to proactively give her that chance to have another moment, another opportunity to say goodbye once I am gone, in hopes of mitigating the gulf that my absence may create in her life. I need her to know that my life has been both full and fulfilling; and culminated in watching her grow into the beautiful person that she is. Please know how much I love you, now and forever.

And, mom, I love you; I will get 'the rest of the story' when I see you.

Introduction

Many people have told me that I should write a book; the problem was that I also heard that you should "write about what you know." I know myself, and I would not have the attention span necessary to maintain a storyline, details and all, throughout an entire book; I sometimes have trouble finishing a conversation. I cannot expound on grand philosophies; I can only write about my own experiences and my perceptions regarding them. However, without finishing my life, at which time it would obviously be too late, there would be no logical beginning, middle or end to the story, and that just did not make sense to me.

When I was young, somewhere in my early- to mid-teens, I was introduced to a theory of time as not a linear sequence, but as a series of random non-sequential moments. I am sure someone out there knows the name of this theory; I do not. I get lost in all the here-to-day-gone-tomorrow theories of science and physics.

Recently I had an epiphany; by applying this non-linear theory to the process of writing, I have exponentially increased my enthusiasm for writing my disjointed biography. I can tell each 'story' as a stand-alone subset to the whole and allow the reader to assemble the parts on his or her own.

In essence, I created a 'do-it-yourself' autobiography!

I began penning random thoughts and experiences, each important in some way to me. Each chapter its own complete story, and all of them woven together help comprise the larger story: the story of my life. There is no beginning, there is no middle and, thankfully, there is yet no end. I invite you to read at your leisure, and in your own chosen order. I present them alphabetically, but then again, that is my background; you choose yours.

My hope is, at a minimum, to keep you mildly entertained; my goal is to share a quirky perspective of the treasures I have discovered on my daily journey through life that created thoughts, feelings, or impressions significant enough to carry with me throughout the years and offer them to you.

I thank you for the opportunity to share my thoughts with you. Please enjoy!

The 72-Hour Day

There is little that demarks the beginning of a pivotal day in your life. Nothing sets off an alarm, nothing warns you that 'something big' is coming; contrarily, oftentimes, the pivotal day begins pleasantly.

Such a day occurred when I lived in Missouri. We had moved there to begin our entrepreneurial business of breeding animals; Great Danes while awaiting our tropical birds to produce chicks. We spent most of our time building a 'barn' ensuring it would be easily convertible to a home, should our enterprise fall flat, and taking care of our livestock. We had seven Danes, thirty assorted tropical birds, and then our 'pets': five cats and one malamute, mine, leftover from a previous version of my life.

This day began wonderfully. Three of our females had given birth successfully, and the litters ranged from 10 to 18 days old; young enough to still be ugly (in a cute sort of way) and old enough to have developed some engaging personalities. That day, two of our neighbors who were becoming friends came to visit, and I took them into the 'barn' to see the pups. I was in there earlier and all the puppy rooms were clean and freshly watered, and they had their first round of worming.

I told them about my favorite in all three litters, "Crescent Man". He was a male fawn with a black, rather than white, backward crescent moon on his chest. He was the largest of the entire litter, and he had easily and firmly wormed his way into my heart! I took them over to see Crescent Man. How odd; he did not seem to be in the pen. I counted the puppies; in that pen there should have been, and were, ten puppies. But I did not see a large fawn: where was he?

I lifted the pups up one at a time, until I saw a black crescent. Oh, my heavens! What happened to this baby? He was scrawny! At this age, with the large number of puppies Danes have, he should have been about one to two pounds. Crescent Man had been larger, but still only a little over two pounds; this puppy weighed, possibly, one pound!

I began looking for all the other puppies in the litter that I had come to know, and universally it looked as though they had lost a lot of weight, since just that morning! I looked at the other pens containing the litters: same story. Then I noticed diarrhea, in all the puppy pens. In my panic, I had not noticed that. This made no sense as I had wormed them that morning!

I honestly could not tell you what happened to our friends. At some point, I am guessing they just realized that our plate was full and decided the only way they could help was to leave. I ran to get my husband, and when he saw the state of all the puppies, he immediately accused me of poisoning them with the worming formula.

"Really, Gary? You honestly think that worming them caused this? Or are you just, once again, pointing fingers, as you are wont to do?" I thought to myself.

Regardless of how well we got along, the bottom line is we still had twenty-seven sick puppies, and we did not know with what. As quickly as they were deteriorating, we had to do something, and it needed to be done soon!

I must explain a bit about the area in which we lived. I had worked at one of the Ameritech subsidiaries prior to moving here, and they had 'warned' me that this area of Missouri worked on the POTS system. As Ameritech is known for creating acronyms that mean nothing to anybody else, I asked, "What is a POTS system?" It stands for "Plain Old Telephone System". *[Really? There's an acronym for that?]*

This POTS system had only a few private lines available at a premium; the rest of us peasants were on the party-line system. The phone rings and, in our case, there were seven distinct rings, each 'assigned' to a specific family on that line. Not that it would stop anybody from picking up their phone to listen anytime it rang (and believe me, they did), so any one or all seven families were privy to whatever was said on that line. We needed to keep that in mind, especially as we were already considered 'outsiders' in the community. This will come more into play later but suffice it to say we knew discretion was paramount to our survival in this community.

There was a vet that lived, literally, at the end of our lane. It was seven miles from our place into town, and he lived and practiced at the intersection leading into town. We suspected that whatever this was might be a little out of his league, so we opted to take a couple of the pups to a "big city" vet in Poplar Bluff. Believe me, this was a tough call as we were incredibly low on funds, but these puppies were our stock in trade, so we needed to get to the bottom of this issue, and quickly. We already had a couple of deaths in the litters, and there were a lot more that seemed imminent.

My husband stayed home to tend to the sick puppies while I drove the hour to the vet. *En route*, we lost Crescent Man. I had also brought the only two remaining littermates of ten from one of the litters who seemed to be in the worst shape of all the puppies. Because Crescent Man was already gone, I opted for the vet to perform a necropsy on him (that is an animal autopsy, for those of you who were curious; they do not use the term "autopsy" for animals), in order to more accurately and quickly diagnose the issue(s) to help the survivors.

According to the vet, this little guy's guts had been ravaged; the amount of damage shown in the tiny expanse of his life was astounding to me! This puppy had fought, and fought hard, to stay alive; but in the end, he was not able to do so.

The vet diagnosed giardia, a bacterial water-borne disease that mimicked parvovirus. The other two puppies I had with me, a male and female fawn, were in ghastly shape. He medicated both, put the female on an IV and instructed me as to what to do with the IV at home. He pretty much wrote the male off, telling me that if the medication helped, he should improve, but he was not giving much hope for his survival.

Then he gave me these itty-bitty pills that I was supposed to cut into quarters to dose the surviving puppies. Cut them into quarters, crush them into a powder and then somehow get them down the throats of puppies that were lethargic, when they were not throwing up or pooping explosive diarrhea. And who had no interest in food or water. Great, no problem – I got this.

Then he told me that in our spare time we needed to bleach down the entire kennel and house, as giardia is highly contagious to all animals. He may not have said it exactly that way, but that was how I heard it. And we needed to do that in such a way that our entire stock of tropical birds, housed in the other half of the barn and are sensitive to 'normal' cleaning products, did not burn their air sacs from bleach. No biggie, just another day in paradise!

Bottom line, we were looking at quite a few 30-hour days just to get done what we needed to do for the animals' survival. Then I remembered my husband's sister and her two young daughters, both of whom had severe allergies to animals, were coming for a visit on Monday. His sister had opted to stay with us, rather than at the motel in town, so that we could spend some time together. This nightmare had begun this morning, Saturday; it was only mid-afternoon, and I was already exhausted!

Overwhelmed with what needed to be done for our animals, I realized we had 48 hours to get our 16-year-old 'tip-out' trailer in a fashion ready to receive allergy-sensitive guests. Clean the very same trailer that, until very recently, had housed all our animals as we finished the 'barn'.

When I got home with the puppies, the news, and the instructions, I begged and pleaded for my husband to call his sister and to try to get them to cancel their trip, or to at least get them to agree to stay in the town's motel. He would agree to neither of those options, at which point I decided it was his problem; I had a barn full of sick, and potentially exposed, animals to deal with and to protect, and they were my priority.

I took those miniscule pills and quartered them. I ground them each down individually, and basically dosed according to relative remaining size; the largest quarter would go to the largest puppy, and so on and so forth down the line. It was a grueling, fastidious process, but I got it done. Some of the puppies perked up a bit, but some, unfortunately, expired. I kept watch throughout the night and dosed them again according to instructions. Then I noticed something odd; the puppies that had shown fewer symptoms began eclipsing the sick ones in death, while some of the sicker ones seemed to improve.

Please, God, do not tell me we are dealing with something else, besides?

Before we moved, we had a wonderful relationship with our vet. He had given his personal number to us, in case of emergencies; I had a sneaking suspicion this qualified. This is where the party line situation plays into the story: if we were going outside our new community for advice, publicly stating that we did not have confidence in the professionals within our new community, we would have to go elsewhere to place the call. We had to drive an hour away to a different town in order to call our old vet to get medical advice.

When he found out what medication had been prescribed for our newborn puppies, he went ballistic. He said that medication was problematic to give to dogs even a year old; he would never prescribe it for newborns! He told us we needed to immediately flush the survivors' systems with charcoal to de-tox them. He asked us a few more questions, and determined that our puppies did, indeed, not even have giardia; they had parvovirus. And for parvo, at that time, there was no cure, nor even a treatment.

Now it was simply a wait-and-see game. Flush their systems of the poison we had given them, try to keep them hydrated and comfortable, and see who could survive. It was fortuitous that we were in a larger town where we were able to quickly locate and purchase the necessary items and return home.

We lost more puppies that day. We lost the little girl on the IV in our living room. I had given up on her brother surviving, so I forewent any of the meds at all for him, including the incorrect one, and just carried him around with me and showed him all the things he would not see in the future; the grass, the sun, and all the beauties of the world God provides.

The body count grew and grew, and yet, my little guy hung on. I could tell he was becoming weaker, but I was determined that he would not die alone; that was about the only thing left I had to offer him. By Sunday night, I could no longer keep my eyes open, and I fell asleep on the couch, puppy in my shirt on my chest.

At about five in the morning, a thunderstorm rolled through the area. We lived on the hillside near a gully, and the storm washed through that gully. It was beautiful, in the country as we were, to stand outside on the porch and watch the storm pass. I showed it to my baby, holding him 'papoose style' to keep him warm, and told him that the angels were bowling, and that soon he would be able to watch them for himself.

After the storm, dawn broke into a beautiful day. I took my little charge into the barn to assess the damage there. A higher body count; how sad. But the good news was that the survivors now seemed energetic. I cleaned the pens, and with nothing to dose them for anymore, just gave them some attention.

It was time now to try to clean the trailer of animal dander. Talk about a fool's errand! But I do not have it in me to be insensitive to my guests, so I endeavored. By the time they arrived, thankfully late in the afternoon, I had just finished the last room: the bathroom. Between bleaching down the barn and 'de-allergizing' the trailer, I had scrubbed until my fingers could do no more; indeed, I had developed a bit of blood poisoning from scrubbing with bleach in ungloved hands. I know, unwise, but that is what I had done.

I was so sleep deprived that I remember little about his sister's visit, other than she seemed to decide that she was on vacation, and that it would be up to us—actually, me—to watch her kids for her. I had alternate plans. As she "unleashed" her kids in the trailer, I used that time to do 'chores' that needed to be done, knowing full well that neither my husband nor anyone in his family would volunteer to help, leaving me blessedly alone.

As tired as I was, 'alone' was enough; I did not have to think, I did not have to converse, I could just 'be'. Me and my puppy.

Ultimately, of the 27 puppies we had in the three litters, only thirteen survived; he was one of them. He was the sole survivor from his litter.

I often wonder if it was because I had given him up to the Lord to take, and shown him unconditional love in the meantime, or if he was just made of a constitution such that his body was able to handle the abuse and survive. Personally, I think it was the former; God does work miracles, we just need to learn to recognize them.

The Abduction

Say what you will about Jane Byrnes' mayoral competence, but the lady sure knew how to throw a party! Until her administration took control, Chicago struggled in its ability to capture a large audience for its events; Ms. Byrne taught Chicago how to do it.

The first time I attended a Chicago Independence Day celebration (traditionally held on July 3rd), the event, under the Byrne administration, had morphed into a full week of Taste of Chicago as the preliminary, culminating with the fireworks and the 1812 Overture as the finale on the 3rd. I worked that day, and a group of us planned to meet after work and walk over to the lake to secure a decent spot to view the fireworks.

The downtown streets were closed by default on the 3rd; they may have not been officially closed, but pedestrians simply overtook the downtown streets and there was little that traffic could do to combat the situation. Oftentimes, realizing they were trapped anyway, the occupants of the cars would just park where they were, climb out and take a seat on their roof or hood to enjoy the show.

My friends, Sharon, Jackie, Erika, and I, were walking down Jackson Street toward the festivities, when my right elbow was abruptly clasped, and I was spun around. I faced four Japanese tourists, all men and all equipped with cameras. They spoke little English but pointed to their cameras and said: "Picture: American Blonde. Picture."

Although camera-shy by nature, I realized my friends were quickly fleeing as we spoke, and there would be little possibility of finding them if I lost them in this crowd. I deferred to the gentlemen's wishes and allowed them to snap a picture or two then made a hasty retreat to locate my friends; also, maybe to chastise them a bit for allowing it to happen!

When I caught up with them, I asked if they had even missed me? I received three blank stares in return; then I realized they had no clue I was gone – for any length of time! Some defense team they were! I told them what had happened, and not one of them of them had noted my absence; to add insult to injury, I had been mid-sentence in telling a story that remained unfinished.

I am not sure if that speaks louder to my caliber of friends, or my storytelling abilities; I guess I will leave that to you!

The Angel on my Shoulder

There have been times in my life that I have thought to myself, "After this incident, I really should not be alive right now." But there I was, and in general, I had enjoyed myself. Ages ago, I determined that I must have a guardian angel sitting on my shoulder; really, there was little other explanation.

There was a clear illustration of this one night when I was in my early twenties. I ran around with a group of people who liked to party. Although I never got into drugs, I certainly have had my share of alcohol, as had most of my friends, and had occasionally combined that with driving. Back then, that did not carry the unforgiveable social stigma as it does today; contrarily, it was quite common.

We planned on bar hopping in the northwestern suburbs. The nicer bars for my gay friends back then, without going downtown, were about an hour northwest of me; since I loved to drive and I enjoyed their bars, I did not mind.

We gabbed and danced all night. We were out at one of their bars and I was enjoying myself, watching all the outrageous dancing and the drama surrounding me. At about 1:00 AM, I decided that it was time for me to head home; especially considering that it was (1) a weeknight and I worked the next day, and (2) close to an hour drive for me to get home. Oh, and of course (3) I was a little tipsy; maybe more than a little bit.

I said my goodbyes and got into my car. As usual, during most of the drive I was on autopilot. From beginning to end of any trip in which I drove, and I drove a lot, I was lucky to remember any specific part of the ride because autopilot would kick in.

But this night was different; about ten blocks from home, I was heading toward an intersection that I knew to be a blind intersection from the south. There was a stop light at the intersection, but an apartment building on the southwest corner blocked visibility from the south when eastbound, which I was, and trucking along at a (probably) "higher-than-allowed" speed, considering it was 2AM in sleepy suburbia on a weeknight.

I realized my foot was depressing the brake. At first, I was confused, because I did not remember thinking I should stop; on the contrary, I looked up and saw I had a green light, and I remember thinking to myself, *"I have the green light, and the right of way."* Truthfully, I spoke to my foot and asked, "What are you doing? Stop it!"

My car completed its stop as I reached the green light. A car, imperceptible to me before, careened through its red light at about 70 miles per hour, or at least so it seemed to me.

Shell shocked, I breathed a sigh of relief, looked up and said, "Thank you."

That was my first confirmation that I had a guardian angel who took care of me, despite myself.

The Arrival

My entire family was born in the same little hospital in the same little town except for me; I was born at home, and in a different state. Oh, and over a toilet.

My dad was finishing his master's degree at the University of Kansas, and my parents lived in the married students' housing. My brother is exactly two years and one day older than I, which seemingly explained why my mom woke up with 'gas pains' the day after my brother's second birthday party. But she quickly realized that they were, indeed, not gas pains; I was just anxious to greet the world!

She asked my dad to call for an ambulance, but the hospital was forty minutes away. While he was requesting the ambulance, she realized that he might be better off getting some instructions, because "this kid was not going to wait!" That was me, always in a hurry. That is, once I had decided. I could deliberate and vacillate with the best of them; but once I reached a decision, it was full steam ahead, there was no stopping me.

Unfortunately for me, my mother was a pragmatist, and did not want to have to clean the sheets when there was a perfectly acceptable toilet waiting to flush the mess away; fortunately for me, my dad was a good catch. Can you imagine that being your initial view of the world? *[Although this could certainly explain a lot.]*

Things did not necessarily get better from there. Having already greeted the world, as well as the porcelain goddess, the ambulance took us to the hospital. My mother had not passed the afterbirth, so we were still 'attached' when the ambulance arrived (what a comfortable trip for my mom). Between taking a surprise trip as well as me being slightly premature, my mom had no chance to pack a bag; as a result, she had no change of clothes, including undies, with her. One of the nurses felt compelled to lecture her about the virtue of modesty! *[I mean...really?]*

Back in the '50s, when they had come so far making strides in medicine, a baby who was born at home, outside the benefit of a 'sterile environment', was considered 'contaminated'. Being a contaminated baby, they placed my bassinette right outside the nursery, in the hallway, where I was free to contaminate only visitors and staff, not the elite sterile babies.

My mother, afflicted likewise with the same disease of "outside contamination", was not allowed to have a roommate, lest she infect her sterile roommate. Following common sense, one would think: *I am contaminated, she is contaminated, we are contaminated with the same germs; could we possibly be in the same room together, contaminating each other?* That answer was apparently, no.

But before you feel too sorry for me, my mom told me that I loved the situation. She said that everyone who walked down that hallway stopped, talked to and paid attention to me. More than I can say for those elitist little prissies behind the window in the nursery–Ha!

In the end, my dad was written up in the college paper as being the 'hero' (my hero, certainly).

Later in life, as I read the newspaper clippings and heard my mom's version of the story, my thought was: "*My mom delivered a baby, in the*

50s, without benefit of doctor, epidural or anesthesia; I raced into the world facing the gaping maw of a porcelain goddess, and my <u>dad's</u> the hero?"

Not that I do not think he was, but could we put a little perspective on this?

The Award

*H*ome ownership is not for sissies!

I have always felt, and have no reason to believe it was reciprocated, that my dad and I made a great team working on houses. It was a perfect partnership: I would buy a 'fixer-upper' with all the dreams and visions in my head, and he would fix it up for me. Not necessarily exactly the way I might have done, but he did add some decent augmentation to my ideas. At times.

Victorian homes are my passion, as well as the bane of my existence! If you ever feel the need for an exercise in futility, try fixing up a Victorian home. The old "two-steps-forward, one-step-back" (or more) rule always applies. And frankly, you should count your blessings if you are able to keep it down to one step back!

The last Victorian I purchased my stepchildren 'affectionately' referred to as the "Slanty Shanty", due in no small part to the condition of the front porch. It was slanted, yes, by design for drainage purposes. However, that may have been exacerbated by the foundation of the porch needing a bit of attention. And the ceiling was caving in, just a little; and there was a portion of the porch deck that we needed to avoid, for fear of dry rot. But other than that, it was great.

And there was a swing!

When the time came to repair the porch, nothing less than a full tear-down would be appropriate. So, I started looking for 'replacement' parts. At some point, someone had rebuilt the porch with craftsman flair for a geometric design; I needed to find some embellishment to bring the 'Painted Lady' back to life!

I found some turned rails, as well as columns, creating the basis for my design. Once I chose those and the handrail, we put the old wooden screen doors we found in the attic back on the double door entry; after my dad refinished and re-screened them, of course. What a difference that alone made on the appearance of the house!

I also wanted a true skirt, not the pre-made latticework deal that most people settle for nowadays. A unique skirt: simple, just 1" x 1" boards placed vertically about an inch apart from each other across the underside of the porch deck; simple, and elegant.

The doors we reattached had a cut-out design running horizontally through the midsection, and I thought it may serve aesthetics well to carry that design through the skirt of the porch. I designed a 'frame' to run across the skirt of the porch, front and sides. It was a simple four-inch-tall plain, framed board, and I was going to paint that same design on it. But he did not do that.

For his convenience, he only did the framework on the front skirt, telling me that nobody would see the sides, anyway. I consoled myself with the old "beggars can't be choosers" adage. For the most part, that placated me. I busied myself with making the best of a 'bad' situation (not really: it was still a 100% improvement, if not more).

Detail of Spindles and Skirt

During this renovation, I received a rather 'suspect' letter in the mail. It was, to my mind, a bad copy of a letter stating that our house had somehow mysteriously received an award. *Really? And how? I had never entered it in anything. I was not even aware of any contests!* The letter was written as though it was being sponsored by our city.

I called City Hall the next day to let them know that someone was perpetrating a scam on their residents. I told them about this bogus award I supposedly received, and they asked me my address. I told them, and they said that no, the house really had received an award.

I asked how that could be, as I was not even aware of the contest. She told me that one of their secretaries walked past my house each day and was enjoying watching the progress; she was the one who entered it in the contest. *Can they do that?* This was how it was entered, and they determined that ours was the "Best New Construction on a Residential Home" for that year. Cool!

I co-owned the 2-flat with a friend, Caryn, who lived downstairs. Although my dad could not be there, Caryn and I attended the award ceremony. We even received a $100 gift certificate to the local hardware store, and a small brass plaque honoring the award, to be housed at City Hall.

As the years passed and my father's eyes and hands began to betray him (right before the rest of his body did), I selected some before and after pictures of my award-winning house, and I retrieved the small brass plaque honoring it from the city, to incorporate into a montage for him. I had it professionally matted and framed for him to hang on his wall to show off at his new residential living community apartment.

I presented it to him on Father's Day, and it was a real boost to his ego; it was a physical manifestation of one of his many accomplishments for him to show others. He took pride in all he created throughout his lifetime. There are many decks, additions, renovations, even an entire home, that can be attributed to him. Personally, I had been the recipient of a couple of decks, a porch, miscellaneous projects and a few remodeled rooms at the hands of my father.

But the award? There was no question: nobody could take that away from my father; that was all his!

Award Winning Porch

The Bad Penny

My world was falling apart.

I was in the midst my second divorce, and I had to find a home for not only me, but for my 2-year-old male Great Dane, my 8-year-old female Malamute, and my green wing macaw. There were not many options moving back to Chicago with this menagerie; I needed to cull the herd.

I knew that I was limiting my choices by taking them in the first place, but they were the ones to whom I was most closely attached, and the reason my marriage was crumbling was that he was abusive, not only to me, but to the animals as well. I wanted to bring as many of our animals as possible with me to ensure that they would not be abused, even if it meant I had to find them alternate homes. And that is just what I planned to do.

My first attempt was to network. We had been breeding Great Danes, so I had some confidence that I would quickly find a home for my beautiful 2-year-old boy. It was the Malamute I was concerned about, being eight years old, and she did not get along with other dogs, especially Great Danes. Keeping the two of them was out of the question; one or the other, maybe, but not both.

It was through one of my Dane contacts that I found a home for the Malamute. Not optimal, as the guy wanted her to 'guard' his junk yard, but at least I was not going to have to put her down, which was the option I felt was most likely for her, between her temperament and her age. The only caveat he had was that he did not want me visiting her. He was the brother of a friend of mine, Sue, so I was reasonably certain she was going to a good home. Sue assured me that he was just a very jealous person, and that it would hurt him if she showed me any affection if I visited. After having her for eight years, chances were that she would greet me affectionately. So, I agreed to let her go: no strings attached.

In retrospect, if I had it to do over, I probably would not have placed her there. But back then I was not aware of all the different scams to get pets as bait for fighting dogs, for medical research, or other sordid motives. And Sue did vouch for him, so it was a tolerable fit at the time for me. Now I could concentrate on placing my male Dane, Sherman Tank.

I ran into a dead end through my contacts in the Dane community, so I began contacting former 'clients'; people who had purchased puppies from us, and for the most part, with whom I had kept in contact.

The first lead was a woman who lived in Chicago; single, like me, and she had a female brindle, just like Shermie. I took him over to meet them, and he liked them both. The woman even had the same name as I did at the time (at least, the one I was getting rid of), and blonde hair styled similarly to mine. I was happy with the placement, so we came to an agreement. I never put a price on him, my intention was to just place him in a good home, but I was not willing to sign his papers over to a new owner until we knew it was permanent.

I left Saturday afternoon feeling confident I had made a great placement for him.

Sunday morning, I received a call from her. It seems she was renting, and her apartment had a 'no pets' clause. I guess Great Danes are not easy to hide from your landlord, so adopting a second one was not an option for her. I went to pick him up, and he behaved as though he had been on a great adventure; he was happy to see me again!

I received a second lead, again from Sue who had helped me place my malamute. Her Great Dane was from a line on Sherman's mother's side renowned for its gentle and patient temperament; she found a woman who was dying to have a Dane from his line.

I spoke with the woman, and without even meeting Shermie, she described my baby to a "T"! I was thrilled to be able to place him in a home where he was so wanted and understood!

Except it did not turn out that way. She wanted to meet me at her local high school, which I guess being a single woman I could understand. Shermie did not take to her, though, he did not take to her *at all!*

Even though I had my own misgivings, having watched his reaction to her, I wanted to give her the benefit of the doubt and give him the best chance for a home. She told me she would love to have him, but I said I would need to see where he would be living.

We trekked over to her home, and to say I was underwhelmed would be an understatement. She had a lot of closed doors in her home, and I could hear dogs behind them. Coming from a place where you would be accosted by as many as seven Great Danes as soon as you walked in the door, all getting along and all free to do as they pleased, this seemed rather odd to me. She had all these Great Danes, and not one was allowed loose to live in the house? Danes are 'people' dogs, and they need to be with their people.

As I looked around, I noticed how depressing the place was. I could not pinpoint anything in particular; it was just an overall impression and gut feeling. But I knew this was not the new home for my baby; he accompanied me home.

It is important to emphasize that Shermie and I had been together since he was four weeks old, and he went everywhere I went; we were, for the most part, inseparable. The first time we were apart for any length of time was when my marriage began to go south, and I came back to Chicago to look for a job and a place to house my zoo, should I be able to find such a place. Each time I placed him and 'gave' him away, or even just feeling out prospective homes, I had already said my goodbyes as though we were going to separate forever, and I was fully prepared each time to leave him if the situation was right.

Emotionally, I had already said my 'final' goodbyes to the same dog twice; and even though I got him back and was happy for that, it made it even more difficult because I knew there would be a 'next time', and I dreaded it!

Then I received a lead through a far-western suburban Dane club that a woman would like to meet Shermie. Because of the distance involved, this time I did a more thorough phone interview, and I really liked her. She was willing to drive the hour to meet him, so she did. And she showed up with 'the boyfriend'. I immediately disliked him, but they were not living together so I gave her the benefit of doubt that she would wise-up.

Shermie liked her and even liked him, so I was willing to give it a try. They took him away on a Tuesday, and by Friday the boyfriend was nagging me for his paperwork. I explained that I had no problem signing his papers over as soon as I knew for sure it was a permanent home, but this was already his third "permanent" placement, and I wanted to ensure his permanent status before I officially signed him over. Begrudgingly, he allowed for that point.

It was a good thing, too, because two days later I received a call from her.

It seems that, although they were boyfriend/girlfriend, he was the one who really wanted Shermie. And I guess his wife was not so thrilled about that. Yes, you read correctly: his wife. That is why she had placed the original call to me. In addition, she wanted to return him because he had heartworms, and her relationship with her boyfriend was deteriorating [*maybe it has something to do with that wife-thing? Just saying…*].

In Missouri, we kept all the dogs on heartworm preventative. In my haste to leave, I did not think to grab any when I left, and I had enough of my life crumbling around me that I did not have the presence of mind to contact my vet for some. My bad! Because now my baby had heartworms, and no home.

I arranged to meet her at a truck stop in the southern suburbs. Unfortunately, even though their relationship had apparently soured, he was the one who brought Shermie to me. I am not entirely sure why he seemed so angry with me, but I remember feeling more than once that I was in danger. That truck stop is still there, and to this day when I see it, I cringe.

He did, however, return Shermie, unharmed and without incident. Once again, Shermie simply behaved as though he had been on a great big adventure and was happy to be back with mommy.

My heart was broken. Now, not only did he not have a home, but I had to decide whether to treat him. At that time, the treatment was brand new, and rather inhumane, in my opinion; it was a difficult procedure for them to survive, expensive, and mandated intensive in-home aftercare. I was not willing to spend the money or put him through that if there was no place for him to go.

I also knew that, with the right owner, it could be a potential bonding experience for them.

My parents had moved to the home they purchased for retirement, about three hours away. I was living in the house in which they had raised us; they had a handshake agreement with friends of theirs from England to eventually purchase the home. In the meantime, I came with the deal. I lived in the attic with my malamute (now gone) and my Great Dane, rent free.

These people were not 'dog people'. They were not anti-dog; they had just never experienced life with dogs and were obviously uncomfortable around them. And with two small children, the size of my dogs was especially intimidating to them. And although I was now 'down' the malamute, the Dane kept returning, like a bad penny!

This last return was the final straw for my father. I came home one day and found that he had come to take Shermie to try to find a home for him out in their area. My parents had moved to a small town in a beautiful area with lots of farms and they knew a lot of people; and my dad admitted to me they could not watch my heart break one more time.

They were also fond of Shermie, so I have no doubt that played into their decision. But it would enable me to concentrate on getting my life back on track, rather than continually chase potential homes for Shermie. I still had to find a job, an apartment and finalize an out-of-state divorce; all of which demanded my attention.

Within the week, my dad called to tell me they had placed Shermie with one of my dad's friends, Kevin. He had heard about Shermie from his dad, so he stopped by to see if he liked him, which he did. But my parents were not home, so he decided to take Shermie to his house to see if he could pass the "chicken and horse" test. Shermie was supposed to leave the chickens alone, as they raised them for meat, and not aggravate or chase the horse.

Shermie passed both with flying colors! He ignored the chickens and ran out into the field to play with the horse, which was reciprocated. Kevin never brought him back; from thereon out, Shermie had a new home!

I arranged for the heartworm treatment to be done out there, convenient to Kevin. The vet said it had been a mild case, maybe just one worm, so Shermie was out and about in no time. And it had helped created a closer bond between him and Kevin. It was hard-won, but well worth it; and the best part was that I could still visit my baby anytime!

Shermie with new owner Kevin's son, Rob

Shermie and mommy

The Boss

I was twenty, and on my way! I had my first full-time job, and I was excited! I was yet to find out just how the world works, and how naïve I was, in certain regard. To my mind, I knew I knew everything; I just had to prove that to the world!

My first day on the job: I was pumped!

I arrived early, punched in, only to discover that I was being immediately sent to a clinic for a physical exam. Nobody told me about this, and my experience with doctors to date was less than impressive; I had a long way to go to find one that I respected.

In my car on my way to the clinic I debated whether to go or to just blow off the job. Ultimately, I figured I had come this far, I may as well give it a whirl. And, who knows? Maybe this would be the doctor that would win me over. It was not.

I survived the physical, got back to work, began meeting people and learning my job. I was a receptionist; I had no practical experience, but the one thing I did know as a recovering teenager: I was good at phone!

The job could be mind-numbing. Answer calls, direct people to the right people/place, etc. I would get an interesting call occasionally, "Hi, I'm calling about the ad in the paper about the helicopter for sale?"

Huh? It turned out that call was legit; the owner of the company did have an ad in the paper to sell his helicopter, as well as 'his and hers leer jets'. It seems to me that if I wanted to sell something, and I ran an ad in the paper, I would make sure the person answering the phone knew what was going on, and what to do with those calls. I hate to throw some common sense into it, but I am just saying.

In case you had not already surmised, the owner of the company was successful. He had, along with his helicopter and leer jets, a fleet of 17 collectable cars: Mercedes, Jags, etc. As far as I knew, it was just him and his wife. I could not figure on why they needed so many cars, and I thought it would have been more of a pain than anything to maintain that fleet. But then again, what do I know?

My attitude was not then, nor is it now, the typical 'corporate' attitude. My job was slow enough that, even though I picked up some accounting work along with my 'receptioning', I had a lot of free time to study people. This has always been one of my hobbies. Later in life, I realized this study allowed me to quickly and subliminally catch onto people's patterns; and sometimes my mind would make wild corollaries.

The owner was in town for an extended period, an infrequent occurrence, as he did not live in the area; he had twelve manufacturing plants ranging throughout the US, but his home base was his plant in Mississauga, Canada, where he resided. He had been doing some gutter work on a ladder at his home in Deerfield, when, hand to God, he stepped back to assess his work.

And too late, I am sure, he realized that probably was not a good move on his part.

He fell and broke his ankle and was 'grounded' from travel for a few weeks. So, we had the privilege of hosting him for lo those many weeks. Each time he pulled up, with his driver and his crutches, an entire cadre of men would, literally, surround the car wanting to be 'the one' to help him out of his car and into the office; the car would be mobbed by those trying to make inroads with him. While I did enjoy watching the spectacle, I really felt sorry for those men: one, in particular.

I already mentioned my mind works in strange ways enabling me to quickly discern behavioral patterns. This was one of those times that was amusing to me. Whenever "The Boss" would show up, I could see "Mr. B" tucking his tail and laying his ears back in submission. OK, maybe I spent too much time with dogs, but this is what my mind saw him doing. In his defense, he was a German Shepherd (maybe because of the oversized ears?), but a dog, nevertheless. I knew this was just a subliminal pattern I had discerned, but in my mind's eye, this was how it played out; it did keep me amused.

One day during this grounding period, The Boss was sitting on the corner of Mr. B's desk, chatting away, and I was happily filing, within ear shot of their conversation. I overheard The Boss say that his leg made him 'feel like an old woman'.

Well, as a young, know-it-all woman, I resented this remark, and I felt compelled to share those feelings. I walked up to him, and I told him so. Respectfully, but I still made it known that the remark was unduly sexist.

I seriously thought Mr. B was going to have a heart attack, right then and there at his desk! His eyes almost exploded out of his head, and I amused myself watching/imagining his ears flatten to his head, and tucking up his tail (OK, not literally, just in my head); maybe even peeing on the floor a little bit.

The Boss just turned to me, sized me up, smiled and said, "You know, you're right. And I am sorry for the way I said it. But you understand what I was trying to say."

"Yes, I do understand. I accept your apology and thank you for offering it."

All was said and done. It was over. And there was no heart attack!

It was entertaining to watch these types of antics; I never once took this job seriously, and never envisioned I would be there forever. It was a hobby; a way to get my parents off my back about getting a job, although I did meet a few good people there.

One of those was the office manager, Jim. Apparently, I made the mistake of assuming that he was my boss. After all, I reported to him each day, he gave me direction, he trained me, he told me the 'ins and outs' of the office; as a newbie, in my mind, he was my boss.

One day, after I had been there a while, Jim and I were talking, and he made some derogatory remark about me 'kissing up' to my boss. At the time, he and I commuted together, as we lived in the same suburb. I thought he was referring to that situation, so I said, "If you don't want to commute together anymore, hey, that's fine, just let me know! I've got my own wheels and I can drive myself every day!" He told me it was not that to which he was referring.

I was confused by this statement, so I asked him who exactly my boss was, and he asked me to guess. Apparently, not Jim; and I did not think it was his boss, Don, as he had little to do with me. So, I thought and thought and thought, and I came up empty.

I could not figure out who this mystery boss could be to which he was referring, over whom I apparently fawned. I asked for at least a hint, and he told me that I had lunch with him every day.

A light bulb went off: *"But he's the plant manager; I don't work in the plant! I work in the office!"*

"Yes, and to whom does 'The Boss' entrust this place when he is not here? With whom does he check in when he's not here?" Wow! I had never thought of it like that: the plant was the business' life blood.

I sheepishly replied, "Bud, the plant manager?" "Yes."

That changed everything for me! I absolutely had to cut ties with Bud. Until then, I had no idea that he was my 'boss': but I could certainly no longer go out for a sandwich and a beer every lunch with him; my mistake!

When he approached me that day for lunch, I had to say no. He was a little taken back by this, so I told him I had just learned he was my boss, 'the big guy', and I could no longer go out and have a beer with him; I just would not be comfortable drinking a beer in front of my boss. He looked crestfallen, but said he understood.

I got used to wandering around at lunch rather than hang with my "Bud", and life at work was certainly not the same, but I would deal; I found other ways to amuse myself.

I had no idea at the time what a position I had put myself in, in both circumstances; I did not realize that until much later in life. But to both their credit, they understood and took it well. It never did affect our working relationship. And Bud and I still enjoyed each other's company in the office.

I ended up not working there long, anyway, but these situations had nothing to do with that; it was time to move on and I left on my own terms. I have nothing but respect, still, for 'The Boss' and for Bud, and how they each responded to me. I am glad that I spoke my mind, and I wish more of the people there were like those two; but it certainly was an introduction into the labyrinth of office dynamics, and office politics, as well.

And there would be more to come on those subjects later in life; of that, I was sure!

The Bouquet

*A*dolescent romance is a mystery – especially to adolescents! My first attempt at "true romance" had turned instead into an adolescent nightmare of sorts. My ex-boyfriend, Scott (and I could not yet believe I had an "ex") had found a new "love", Denise, making us instant rivals.

Especially as his sister, Jane, and I were still good friends, and we would run into each other occasionally at their house. Except, I really did not understand his relationship with Denise. You see, we would not run into them as a *couple*, we would run into them as a *threesome*: her little sister, Diane, was their constant companion. I did not comprehend that, nor did I want to delve into it, but I digress!

Denise and I did share a fondness for "cruising", and at some juncture during most cruise nights, our paths would cross. It generally ended up in a competition of sorts in which, in my humble opinion, I would *smoke* her!

One night, we were cruising with our regular crowd after seeing a play my two drama friends were in, and they were accompanying us. I drove my parents' station wagon which, at that time, had the furthest back-seat-facing-backward style, and my two drama friends, Susan and Michelle, were in that seat with bouquets they had received from performing in the play that night.

We happened upon Denise, and my ex was riding as her passenger. I trapped them in an "I" alley; I had lured her into following us down the short end of the alley, then I turned down the long end and she followed. At the very end, I just stopped. She either had to back down the entire alley in a teenage equivalent "drive of shame" or wait it out until I allowed them passage by moving. Janie casually mentioned at this point that it was Denise's birthday.

My mind formed an evil plot, and I asked my florally gifted friends how attached they were to their bouquets. Michelle immediately volunteered hers saying she really was not that attached. I told her I would roll the back window down and asked if she would not mind climbing out the back to give her flowers to Denise, with my birthday regards.

Being dramatically inclined anyway, it was her pleasure to play in my little scenario!

"Happy Birthday, Denise!"

I watched the entire scene play out in the rear-view mirror. The look on Denise's face was absolutely worth the price of admission! And I could see in the mirror that he was likewise mortified.

Good. My work here was done! Michelle climbed back into the car, and we all had a good laugh, then went out for some grub, as all good teenagers do!

Oh, how I miss my carefree, albeit rather nasty, days!

The Buddy

There are times when we all stand in the presence of an angel. If we are lucky, we even recognize it; I was fortunate enough to know.

Watching my father's decades-long decline was difficult; especially as I had been a "Daddy's Girl" (or at least, I considered myself so) all my life. He was at times my confidant, my protector, my provider, my defender, my mentor, and my tormentor; he was all things to me rolled up in one, magnificent daddy-bundle.

About ten years before my parents both passed away, they each individually experienced a health scare, and I vowed to myself that neither one of them would ever wonder if I loved them or appreciated them. I made it a point to travel every other weekend to visit with them, even though it was they who had moved out of town and away from us. But they only had one grandchild, and I wanted to ensure they knew her, and she them. My mother and I had become great friends by this time, and I treasured our visits. But observing my father decline and occasionally watching him take his frustrations out on my mom took an emotional toll on me.

The time eventually came when he could not accomplish the things he once easily achieved; moreover, it seemed he was so far gone that he did not even recognize that fact. That process accelerated after my mother passed away; for although none of us was ready, it was my father who lost his anchor, and his very hold on life. He became a person whom I neither knew nor recognized; and having to travel long-distance to visit with him, to shoulder the day-to-day responsibility for his behavior and his medical needs, while simultaneously working full-time and being a single mom, well, let us just leave it that I was less patient with him than I should have been.

There were times I admit that I even held it against him that, in my opinion, he contributed to my mother's demise, although intellectually I knew there was no more way he could control what happened to him or his body than he could control how my mother responded to it. As the "baby" of the family, I felt that I had been cheated somehow; but then I met my angel.

The receptionist at my workplace, Jackie, became enamored of the stories I told of my long-lost dad. She delighted in his sense of humor and enjoyed hearing of his antics throughout my life. It felt good to talk about my father in a positive light, as that had not happened often as of late. It was good to remember my dad for who he was and how much he had meant not only to me, but to the rest of his family and friends.

She brought a simpler perspective to my relationship with my father making it easier to visit him every other week. Instead of him being a checkmark item on a "To-Do" list to accomplish, Jackie caused me to remember the humor, the love, the kindness and the consideration my dad had always brought to my life; she taught me how to appreciate and cherish him in a new light and gave him back to me, even if just for the moment.

And with the shift in my attitude, I realized that this was the man who raised me, this was the man who stood by me as I changed; as I grew up, and as I did things that might have challenged him, or thwarted him, or that were maybe even downright hateful to him. But he never gave up on me, and I realized that I had given up on him, even though there was nothing he could have done that would have altered what he had become.

Having that realization, I determined that I needed to reacquaint myself with him. No, he was not my dad, per se; but the person he became was important to me because of who he was, and he needed to know that. I will not pretend that the frustration was over, or that it was an easy path for either of us, but I can say that it was worthwhile. And although this was not "my father", he was a fascinating person to get to know.

Jackie looked forward to hearing about his most recent escapades, and she dubbed him "her Buddy"; she became quite protective of him. In response, I realized how much more I enjoyed being with him, accepting him as he was without expectation that he will ever be what I remember, just loving him for who he was in the moment. And when I was able to entertain Jackie with stories of his humorous antics, she aided me to feel a closer bond with him as well.

Because of Jackie, I can view his last years of life with appreciation, getting to know him as a different, but still important, person to me. His sardonic wit survived, although most times it was difficult to understand his words. I realized, especially after he passed, how much Jackie had played a role in my ability to enjoy my father again, and how much I received emotionally from his last few years.

With a simple change of perspective, she enabled me to create cherished memories that I will enjoy the rest of my life. Thank you, Jackie; you are an angel.

The Coat Hanger

"My" car had been out of commission for a full week, and I missed it! But that is what happens when you drop a drive shaft; the car needs a little time to "recuperate".

But, miracle of all miracles, my parents were notified that the car was ready on Friday. The very same day that Sara and I were invited to a party; the first "A-List" party to which we had ever been invited – and a party that would have all our 'crushes' in attendance.

To be fair, she only had a crush on one guy; I had about five. But they would all be there!

And now it was confirmed that we would have transportation! This was so meant to be!

On the way to the party, we picked up our friend Gregg. The party was being hosted by one of the five guys I had a crush on, and although I knew exactly where he lived, in the excitement of the moment and heading there from Gregg's house, I was disoriented. So, I asked him in which direction we should head, and he pointed behind us.

Rather than doing the normal thing and just drive around the block, I decided it would be faster to do a three-point turn. Dumb!

The area Gregg lived in had tall curbs. REALLY tall curbs. And performing a three-point turn as fast as I did (remember – I was going to see all my secret crushes there and I was in a hurry), I ran into the curb. Well, not me exactly: the car did. The curb bent the tail pipe, which made a horrible noise scraping the street, all the way to the party. Not exactly the entrance we had anticipated.

We finally got invited to an A-list party, with all our crushes standing around us, and all I could think about was the darn car and the dread I had at the thought of taking it home.

Apparently, this was obvious, because eventually, the entire party moved out to my car to see if they could help repair it. This was fun. It reminded me of the good old days of barn-raising, where everybody pulled together to help each other out for a common goal. It is just that I felt so very blonde at that moment, and I was humiliated. Even though I saw the camaraderie the situation engendered, I was not feeling it.

One of the attendees, Paul, retrieved his truck and turned it to face my car, illuminating my car with its lights so they could see exactly what I had done. Another party attendee, Tom, got underneath my car to assess the damage, and at one point he wriggled out from underneath, spit out some lawn/sod that had fallen into this mouth, and jokingly asked me, "How many lawns did you drive over?" right before he scooted back under the car. "Just one," I answered.

He emerged again, just to look at me to see if I was joking. I shrugged, and immediately remembered that he knew my dad. Probably most of them did, as my dad taught at our high school, and he kept score at the football and basketball games, as well as the track events. Most of these guys were jocks, but I could not think about that right now! Tom looked at me quizzically, shook his head as if to clear it, then disappeared back under the car. Everybody else just congregated, laughing, drinking and talking, waiting to see what could be done.

Tom asked for a coat hanger, and I remember thinking, *"It's like he's a doctor saying, 'Scalpel' and it appears; except he said, 'coat hanger'.*

It appeared, nonetheless, and Tom eventually emerged, telling me he had fixed it.

I thanked them all for their help, and the party began to migrate back into the house. Sara and I looked at each other and tacitly agreed; we found Gregg and told him that we would just as soon get the car home and call an end to this evening. He understood. He stayed, but he understood.

I drove Sara home, and then proceeded home myself.

I parked the car, facetiously congratulated myself on my triumphant return, and went to bed, immediately erasing the entire evening out of my life. And I mean, I *ERASED* it!

On Sunday morning, my parents came home from church, and my dad asked if anything had happened to the car on Friday. Even that did not trigger anything. I truly had forgotten the entire incident – no, make that I had absolutely no recollection whatsoever of the incident, because I had been so mortified – and answered, in all honesty at the time, "No. I don't remember anything out of the ordinary happening."

That was when my dad absolutely lost it!

He could not believe the service station would fix the tailpipe with a stupid COAT HANGER of all things! Suddenly, in hearing those two words: I flashed back to Tom's request, and then remembered.

And I froze.

Oh, no! He had discovered the 'repair', and suddenly all the humiliation and memory of the horrible evening flowed back to me. And I had already, albeit inadvertently, lied about it!

Not knowing what to do, and not being prepared for this situation (even though I really should have been), I decided to take the route of least resistance. I concurred with him that fixing the tail pipe with a coat hanger was horrible, and irresponsible, and I could not believe that was how 'they' would fix it. Note that I never mentioned the service station; just that it should not have been fixed with a coat hanger.

In a strange way, it felt a little less like I was lying to him. OK, so I had to stretch my imagination a bit, but it worked for me.

And I sent up a little prayer that Tom would not run into my dad for at least a while.

I never did find out what the service station said, but I did not really care to ask, either.

The College Mascot

I am an avid animal lover. Everybody knew it. If anyone in the neighborhood went on vacation, I would probably know because, if they had pets, they called me to take care of their four-legged critters while they were gone. And I loved it! Most times I did not know how they knew me or how they got my number; and frankly, I did not care. I did not even particularly care whether they gave me anything or paid me. In my mind, the more animals that surrounded me, the better!

I knew the neighborhood by the animals. When we lived in our apartment and the kids were all out playing in the alley, there was this one poor black and white dog I noticed and for which I felt sorry. She was always out, always chained near her 'house', just off the alley. I never saw anyone out there with her, I never saw her not there; this was her life.

As the other kids played, I went into her yard, and sometimes even into her house, and kept her company. I talked with her for hours; I never even knew her name, but I loved her.

Later, as my 'territory' expanded, I learned other houses by their animals (dogs in particular, but some exotics, such as a duck). I would visit Donna, the fawn Chihuahua, and talk with her owner for hours. Her owner, Jean, was an older woman who taught me a lot about gardening during this time. I did not mind; I was able to spend time with Donna.

Then there was Georgia. She was the Bassett Hound who lived on the next block. I felt sorry for her because she did not have a yard, only a small cement enclosure. And I am not exactly sure how it began because I did not even know her owner's names, I just started showing up on their doorstep to see if I could take Georgia for a walk. Surprisingly, they always acquiesced.

But Sammy (Samantha) was my favorite. Sammy was the miniature Schnauzer who lived across the street. Sammy and I had something that I did not even have with my own dog. We had a love affair that was legend to her owners. Sammy's 'dad' would walk her, and if she saw me outside, she would strain at the leash to get to me. He would let her go, generally about a block away, and she would come streaming toward me, leash trailing behind, and jump into my arms! I am not sure that even I understood her devotion to me, but I did love it!

And so it went, throughout my life, the black cat that belonged two doors down, the duck that lived across the street, the dog and cat that lived on the next block – I visited them all and spent time with them and their owners.

When I left for college, being without an animal was like going through withdrawal. I was in serious need of an animal fix!

Eventually, I decided to get a guinea pig. My roommate, whom I had not known before our pairing, had pretty much abandoned me for her boyfriend, which left me both animal-less and roommate-less in a foreign environment. "Cricket" was my solution: a little calico-colored Abyssinian guinea pig. She was a little cutie, and pretty much a perfect roommate for me.

As the year went on, and through my absentee roommate's friends, I met a guy. He had a dog, a German Shepherd named Lucky. And a motorcycle. That was enough for me!

He took me on motorcycle rides, and we would take Lucky to the park. Eventually, falling into my old patterns, I began taking her out by myself, and we (Lucky and I) ended up 'rescuing' a little 3+ month old male Irish Setter. I had Lucky in the Grove with me when this anti-social puppy came over to play. He wanted nothing to do with me but was following Lucky and trying to engage in play. Knowing that the frat next to my dorm had Irish Setters, I grabbed him, and we went over to my dorm to call them.

I asked if they were missing an Irish Setter puppy and was told yes. [*Yay! I found his home!!*]

When I responded that I had him, there was a very pregnant pause. "*Him?*"

"Yeah", I said, "I have him."

He said they had lost a six-month-old female, and I looked at 'my' puppy to make sure. I said no – this little guy (and he is a guy!) is about three to four months. Do you happen to know where he belongs?

Nope.

Uh-oh!

So, I hung up the phone. "*Hey, guess who is coming to dinner?*" I thought to myself.

I thought for a while, then contacted the Humane Society. I gave them a full description, and even included the fact that he was wearing a yellow cat collar ("*Really? How could you?*"). Then I called the college newspaper because I knew they had a "Lost & Found" column. I even called the local student radio program, knowing they had a lost and found listing, too.

In the meantime, he went home with Lucky.

Each day I came 'home' to see if anybody had called, and each day my bond with him became stronger and stronger. After about a week, I talked to my boyfriend, Jim, about keeping him and having him live with him while I was in the dorms. He said that was fine, and I began to accept that I had my first, very own real-life dog!

Eight days after I found him, I came home to devastating news. There was a call. And this guy was coming over at 6:45 to claim him. "Did he know about the cat collar?" I asked in desperation. "Yes. And he even knew it was yellow."

I hated him already.

6:45. No show. 6:50. No show. The minutes ticked slowly by as I watched the clock and waited for this man to come devastate my life. At 7:05, I began to have hope. At 7:15, the phone rang again. (*"Darn! He still has our number!"*)

Yes, it was indeed him again. This time, he was a little more forthcoming with me. It was not his puppy (I liked him better already – he was not responsible for the yellow cat collar). The puppy belonged to his roommate, and was an expensive gift from his father, who enjoyed hunting. But, according to him, since the day this little guy came into his life, his roommate had not taken care of him. He left him neglected, assuming others would care for the puppy for him, which the caller had done.

The caller, who never did identify himself, had spent the time between calls #1 and #2 talking to his roommate to find out the progress of his roommate's search. He discovered that his roommate had done nothing to try finding the puppy. The caller asked his roommate that if he located the puppy, could he keep him?

"No! He's my dog, not yours!" the roommate snapped.

That second call was him telling me, if I would promise to give this puppy a good life, as far as he was concerned, I could have him.

O-M-G!!!!! My baby could stay with me!!!!

I was over the moon and was finally officially able to give him a name: McCabe; a family name. My grandmother's maiden name. He was now officially a part of my family! I was so excited!

Finally, my own dog: McCabe!

And then a week later, I got another call.

I guess the roommate's father, who had gifted his son with the puppy, was coming into town. NOW, two weeks later, his roommate was trying to find him. *[I found out that his roommate had named him "Scruffy". Really? For an Irish Setter? How undignified!]*

The roommate called the humane society (that was how the original caller got our number), and someone from there told him that they had received a call about a setter puppy, but that owner had been located and they threw the notes away, as the puppy had never been in the facility (God Bless my caller!). They had nothing else on a setter puppy.

He just called to give us the heads up – I thought he was going to try blackmail, but I guess he had the puppy's best interest at heart.

So, we started taking him out in public only at night – other than that, it was backyard-city for this guy, and supervised, as we had no fence. After a few days, we began to relax again.

And then, we got another call. [*OK, could we just change the number, please?*]

This time, he said his roommate's girlfriend, who apparently lived near Jim's house, told her boyfriend that about the time his puppy was lost, this house near hers seemed to have acquired an Irish Setter puppy. Again, just a "heads up" informational call. Just enough to put me on pins and needles. Again.

Now, I was serious! McCabe went out only at night. He had a white flame on his chest that I shaved off. I did not want any identifying marks remaining on him. I kept him 'underground' for about six months, at which time I decided he had grown to be unrecognizable enough to see the light of day again, although in my eyes, he was both singular and stunning!

I began taking him to classes with me. All of them. We were inseparable, and we both enjoyed it. Except for the time that he threw up in a lecture hall during a lecture; that was not fun for either of us. But for the most part, life was returning to normal.

And then it happened.

I had McCabe with me when I ran into one of my dorm friends. We stopped to talk, and because McCabe was very well behaved, he was not on leash. Of course, he <u>was</u> still a puppy.

As she and I spoke, I noticed across the street, where I needed to pass, a guy was sitting on the building's stoop. Watching McCabe's antics: it was late October, and McCabe had discovered an old garden still containing gourds; he was using them as balls, tossing them in the air and catching them, then running around and through the bushes like a fool, like a puppy!

But this guy, this college-aged guy, was not watching the two statuesque blondes standing there talking; he was laser focused on the dog.

I implored her to stay with me at least until that guy left. But, he remained, and she had to get to class. So, I was left alone, save my precocious puppy, to walk past him.

He was fascinated by the dog. I had convinced myself that this was the original owner, and that, growing spurt aside, he had recognized his dog despite the missing flame. As we got closer to him, he finally looked at me, smiled a very lop-sided smile and said, "Nice dog."

"Thanks!" I said and hurried past him. To this day, I am not sure which one this was, but I think now this was the caller, realizing that he had done the right thing. I hope.

As for McCabe, he did lead a long and happy life with us. He was with us for ten years, and chose a night the entire family was together, hosting a party, to depart from this life. He said his goodbyes to us, curled up in his doghouse, and went to sleep. We all adored him, and for years thereafter, a portion of my heart was missing.

He was such a good boy!

It was a wonderful life with you, McCabe.
I miss my constant companion, rest in peace!

The Conductor

*A*ll of you commuters out there: you will understand!
When you begin a life of commuting, you enter a world of which the "non-commuters" are ignorant. That is not a negative, they just do not realize that, with or without you on it, the train leaves the station at the same time (er...at least, mostly). That is the agreement we have, as commuters, with our mode of transport. And there is not one commuter out there who would not agree that if this is your life-style, you have things timed down to the minute, sometimes even to the second.

You get to know passengers, if not by name, by face. You know who 'belongs' and who does not. You get to know your conductor, and watch him/her in action so that you know pretty much what kind of a person they are; their likes, their dislikes, whether they enjoy their passengers (hint: they call commuter trains 'cattle cars', if that tells you anything), how they collect tickets, etc. And you form an opinion. As human beings, that is what we do, like it or not. This conductor is nice, this one really loves his family, this one is really a player, this one is a tool, and so forth.

Having always lived near the city, I prefer to stand in the vestibule rather than bother to grab a seat. It just seemed more expeditious

– because by the time I choose a seat, sit down, get settled, etc., there is no time to accomplish anything. So, I generally used my commuting time as my social time.

Prior to moving to my new home, I had commuted on a different line. I rode on a train where, in order to be allowed to stand in the vestibule, you (1) had to be a smoker (back in those golden olden days, we tolerated smokers, but segregated them on the train), which I was, and (2) you had to tell a joke. If the vestibule riders laughed, you were allowed to be a standing 'member' (literally) of the vestibule club. If not, you were banished in shame to the interior of the car and relegated to a seat.

I cannot remember what joke I told, but I was allowed membership to be a regular vestibule rider. But this is all background for you on what kind of rider I am: I prefer to be sociable, gregarious, and make friends with the passengers and conductors.

Then I moved. And it was not even just a new train or line that I was on, it was an entirely different railroad and a new station for me; the whole system seemed foreign.

And that is when I got "The Grouch". No one knew what he was really like. He banished all people from the vestibule. He did not allow anybody to stand in 'his' vestibule, and kept himself king of his realm, empty though it may be.

Now, this was a challenge because I still did not like sitting. And, although I had moved to a different train line, the first stop on most trains was my destination. At that point, there was no purpose to sitting. I had to figure out a way to get through to him to allow me to fuel my vestibule habit!

I sat in the car on the stairs leading to the upper deck, simply because it was as close as I could get to the vestibule, without taking up space in his little kingdom. Trying to figure out what made him tick, I watched him every day. And one day, I figured out how to break through to him.

He had finished his rounds earlier than usual and pulled out a book from his pocket. Aha! One of my favorite authors, Og Mandino, and believe it or not, a positive mental attitude speaker! [Really?]

The next morning, I grabbed one of my books written by the same author as a prop (I told you he was one of my favorites; I have, I believe, every single book he has written or co-authored). When he passed me and gruffly asked for my ticket, I exaggeratedly closed my book (I had chosen the one with the author's name written as large as possible on the cover) and feigned searching for my ticket, apologizing as I explained that I was in the middle of this great book by this great author, and had forgotten to get my ticket out and available. At that point, he looked at me, and really *saw* me. He looked at the book and said, "Hey – I'm reading a book by that same author! [Really?] Isn't he fantastic?"

"Yes," I said. "I own all of his books." He took my ticket and went on.

The next day, as I was passing through the vestibule and into the car, he grabbed me by the elbow. We started chatting, initially about the author and his books, and from there we strayed to other topics. Meanwhile, I acted as if I was on my way to sit down, but he insisted that I stay out in the vestibule with him. Well, OK, if you insist!

Soon, I was his vestibule regular, and I began inviting other passengers I knew to join us. Remember, this man had a 'reputation', and they all looked at me like I was nuts. But eventually we had established our core group of vestibule riders, and we even took over the PA system to announce the stops and give the reminders to take your tickets and your personal belongings with you as you exit the train, etc. I was the main PA-er, but I had substitutes lined up, should I be absent.

I have learned that everybody has something to teach, and everybody has something to learn. I put that into action, and made friends of a group of strangers, beginning with "The Grouch". Life is grand!

The Construction Guy

Sometimes, a new frame of reference is all that is needed.

I only need to emerge from the train station, cross a street, and then a bridge to get to work in the morning. For some reason, the city LOVES to have construction on this bridge, and not necessarily very well-advertised.

I prefer to arrive before 7:00 in the morning and have more 'day' at home later to enjoy with my family. At a certain time of year, that means the sun is exactly at the level to peek between high-rises and shine straight down Adams and directly into my eyes, blinding me as I walk east on the street.

While this is a temporary situation lasting only for a week or two, it can be very annoying, and sometimes dangerous, as you really cannot see the traffic – or anything else, for that matter.

One morning as I was crossing the street, I realized we were in "that time of year" that the sun blinded the pedestrians. This morning, the north pedestrian sidewalk crossing was closed due to repair, while the south was open. And, without the ability to see, the construction guy responsible for keeping pedestrians off that sidewalk was getting frustrated and angry with us. After all, there were signs stationed all over informing people the sidewalk was closed. Yet, partially due to being on autopilot but mostly due to being sun-blind, we ignored them.

I unwittingly wandered into his construction site, and boy, he was not going to have it! He shooed me away unceremoniously, and I quickly complied, with apologies.

But as I was walking away, I heard him yell – really yell – at a pedestrian walking behind me. Keep in mind, he was facing west with clear vision, while yelling at all the vision-impaired pedestrians heading east. And he was not necessarily as kind to the person behind me as he was to me.

So, I turned around, walked back to him and tapped him on the shoulder. When he turned to see me (and he was not exactly wearing a happy face!), I said "You know, the sun is literally blinding all of the pedestrians heading east. You could put all the signs out that you want, but with the sun's position, none of us can see any of them."

He turned his head further see what I was talking about. I saw that he understood what I was saying, but he was not ready to admit yet that he had made a "boo-boo". Having spoken my mind, I turned and headed into work.

The next morning, as I was about to cross the street from the train station again, I saw a "Sidewalk Closed" sign – and there was 'my' construction guy. He had moved the sign into the shade, ensuring that people could see it, and was doing a funny dance and pointing to the sign to get people to notice it; and I sensed he was having more success.

When he saw me, he gave me a big ole grin, and waved. Then he pointed at the sign, and I gave him a 'thumbs up', a grin and a nod.

It made me realize how important, and simple, changing your perspective and seeing things from someone else's point of view can be; and I would like to believe it taught him the same!

The Contrast

J was waiting for the call; in my opinion, it was long-overdue. And, although I was expecting it, I was also dreading it. Still, it came as a shock.

My father, who had the misfortune of being both in poor physical condition and of outlasting my mother, his sole caretaker, had finally done it. After my mother's passing, we were fortunate to find a care facility that (1) allowed him independence and privacy, and (2) had a great staff that could be counted on to help him when he needed it.

Eventually, reality and complacence took their toll. My father was, as they described it, 'non-compliant' with therapy, and he had stopped taking his meds. Whether or not that was his intention, that was the reality. As a result, they decided, for his own well-being, he could no longer be a resident where he had lived since my mom passed on; now, he needed to be placed in a nursing home.

I had so many emotions roiling around. I saw my dad, my hero, the core strength from my childhood, the one who would always stick up for me, who rescued me more times than I can remember, look back at me with vacant eyes. And I wondered if he even saw me, my heart broke.

Although he seemed so lucid at times, there were many times that, despite my best efforts, I could not figure out what he was trying to say. Much of that was due to one of his medical conditions, a problem with his throat. But then he would talk about the family who lived underneath him, telling me about their sidewalk and driveway. I pointed out to him that his apartment was on a slab foundation; and I knew he wanted to argue the point, but I think he was still able to follow logic. At least, most of the time.

I was heading down to make the physical move for him. The drive going down there was gorgeous, right up to taking the off ramp into town. Just as I did so, there was a bolt of lightning directly in front of me, a huge clap of thunder, and the skies opened and let out a torrential rainstorm; I could not even see the road!

I thought, *"I checked the weather. It was supposed to be on the cool side, but there was nothing about rain. I only have flip-flops. And, I have my hoodie instead of my rain jacket. Great!"*

I felt like a duck most of the day – sloshing around on my flip-flops going here and there and running errands, tying up loose ends of a life I was not living, but for which I seemed to be currently responsible. Going to the bank, the office supply store for boxes, his old residence for immediate needs; phone charger, changes of clothes, personal hygiene products, and mementos. How was I supposed to pick mementos for someone else's life? But I wanted him to have the creature comforts of home, whatever that meant to him now. He just was not really communicating to me what those were.

I collected a bunch of 'stuff', took it to him and discovered it had to go through 'inventory'. Although they assured me that it would not take long, after two hours of waiting with him for his stuff to clear, I gave up and told him I was going back to his old place to pack some more, now that we had talked, and I had a better idea of what he wanted.

It was 3:00 pm, and I was heading back for that second trip when I realized I had not had anything to eat all day. I had gotten up at 4:00 to arrive at a decent enough hour to accomplish as much as I could. By now, I was seriously thinking of gnawing on my arm a bit, just to hold off starvation!

I contacted one of my cousins in the area and met him and his family for dinner. It was a nice distraction, and the first relaxing thing I had done all day. We lingered, catching up, but they had a meeting to go to at 6:00 pm, so we all left around that time.

Because we sold my parents' home after my mom passed, I occasionally stayed at one of the local inns, and I knew the managers, at least by sight. I walked in and something seemed different, it was subtle, but it was different. No one was behind the desk, and there was an instruction to dial "0" on the phone if assistance was needed, so I did.

When he answered, he seemed a little frazzled, but had his usual cheerful demeanor. As he was checking me in, he realized his phones were down as well as his computer. One by one, the residents were coming down the stairs to report that they had no power, or that some parts of their rooms had no power, while other parts had it.

Then, the fire alarm went off. I looked at him and asked, "How's your day going?" He laughed and told me I was an angel!

He finished checking me in, and I trotted off – fire alarm blaring – to put my suitcase in my room, and to run back to check on my dad. I spent about a half hour in my room, most of it listening to the fire alarm, and on my way out I noticed that a fire truck had arrived, lights and all. How exciting! As I passed the front desk, I asked if I could stop on my way back and get him a cocktail to go, and he laughed!

I got to my dad's new place, and found him in bed, ready to sleep. At 7:10. On the night of the 7th playoff game, in a world series featuring his Cubbies. He had been a life-long Cubs fan and I asked why he was not in the lounge watching the game. He asked, "What game?" I told him, "THE game – the one you have been waiting for all your life! Get out there and watch your Cubbies!" "Oh," he said, "I wanted to see that."

I helped him dress and took him into the lounge for the game. I stayed with him and watched for a while, but in my entire life any Cubs game that I have watched, they have lost. Even I realized they were on a roll that night, so I excused myself to my dad telling him I was tired and had to go get some sleep. In my mind, this would ensure a win for his beloved Cubbies.

Since I now had some extra time on my hands, I decided to stop by the liquor store to find a joke gift to take to the desk clerk at the hotel. I know they make cocktails to go, or cocktails for one, or some such thing, but not being a drinker myself (anymore), I did not know exactly what was available. I must have looked lost in the store, and the saleswoman asked if she could help me find something.

I quickly outlined the circumstance and said that I was looking for kind of a joke gift to brighten his day. She suggested a couple of things that did not seem quite appropriate to me, so then she asked me what he preferred to drink. I said, "He might be an alcoholic, for all I know – I have no idea what he prefers!"

So, she asked where I was staying, and I told her.

"Chuckie-Bear? Are you talking about Chuckie-Bear?" I laughed and said I did not have a clue what his name was, but I did know that it was NOT the general manager, and it was not the lady. She said, "That's Chuck!" and then she took me over to the wine aisle and pointed out his preferred brand of wine.

Although I could appreciate that it would be exactly what he would enjoy, it was no longer a gag gift, so I was less than enthusiastic now about purchasing it. I had to talk myself into it, but eventually (and more because of the lack of options for the gag gift that I had in mind) I bought a bottle for him. She gave me a message to deliver with the wine: "Tell him Lynn says 'hi' and that she's still waiting for her ticket to Ireland!"

I looked at her and said, "Sorry, honey. If he is taking anybody to Ireland, it's going to be me!"

I bought the bottle and headed for the hotel.

Upon entering, the front desk was again unattended. I thought to myself he must still be having a challenging shift!

I made the call to "0" again, and he came out. When he saw me, he smiled. I put the bottle, currently wrapped in a brown paper bag, on the counter, and he smiled broader. He told me I really was an angel, and so nice to think about him. I said, "But you haven't opened the bag."

When he pulled out a bottle of his wine, I thought his eyes were going to pop out of his head. I could see him thinking to himself, *"How in the world did she pick this of all the choices she could have made?"* He looked at me, incredulous, and I said, "Lynn says hello, and she's still waiting for her ticket to Ireland. But if you have tickets you are giving away to Ireland, I would like one, too!"

He laughed and said he would take us both! I bid him goodnight, and he told me he gets off at 11:00; he has a 10-minute drive home, but that this bottle would be uncorked by 11:15! I laughed and returned to my room.

I purposefully stayed away from <u>any</u> news of the baseball game. Indeed, I had no idea they had won – until my daughter texted me! What a gift for my dad to see – I was so happy for him!

I was also having a difficult time sleeping.

To see my father's life ending in this manner was heartbreaking; to melt away from life, bit by bit, with your own body seemingly turning on you and betraying you. I had watched my father, my strength, my hero, slowly decline for fourteen years, that we have noticed. Fourteen years that it had been apparent *to us* that something was not quite as it should be with him; it made me wonder how long it had been since *he* had known that something was wrong.

After a restless night, I got up. Time to really begin digging and sorting through his stuff. And time to have some difficult conversations with him. I already had to explain to him that this was not the temporary move he thought it to be; that he had been permanently displaced from his home because of his medical needs.

Watching my dad leave this way, as contrasted to my mother's 12-hour struggle, gave me a lot of time to think about my own "exit".

My dad's situation reminded me of a line from t.s. elliot's poem, *The Hollow Men*. "This is the way the world ends, this is the way the world ends, this is the way the world ends...not with a bang, but a whimper."

Personally, I prefer the style of William Cullen Bryant in *Thanatopsis*:

> So live, that when thy summons comes to join
> The innumerable caravan, which moves
> To that mysterious realm, where each shall take
> His chamber in the silent halls of death,
> Thou go not, like the quarry-slave at night,
> Scourged to his dungeon, but, sustained and soothed
> By an unfaltering trust, approach thy grave,
> Like one who wraps the drapery of his couch
> About him, and lies down to pleasant dreams.

Such a pleasant image – wrapping yourself up and lying down to pleasant dreams. And, come to think of it, that was how my mother went. She went to bed one night and is still having her pleasant dreams.

Goodbye, mom. Enjoy your dreams. I love you and I will always miss you.

And goodbye, dad. I had missed you for years before you passed; but I am comforted in knowing you are in a better place now. I love you!

The Curfew

I believe my parents were facing the "empty nest" syndrome. I was the baby of the family, but then again, there were only the two of us. So, pardon me if I felt that my impending move to the dorms, a mere three hours away, really did not qualify them for this event; but I could not perceive any alternate explanation.

I had never in my life had an 'official' curfew. As the one with the most access to a car, my parents' philosophy was to allow me discretion and to let me stay out beyond my friends' curfews, enabling me to drive them home. They trusted me, and generally I was home between 1:00 and 1:30AM. This system had worked beautifully for all parties involved, until now.

One night, two weeks before I left for U of I, there was an incident; I do not remember exactly what because it was inconsequential except for the fact that I was home later, apparently much later in their opinions, than I should have been.

The following morning was Sunday, and my dad sat me down for "a talk" to explain to my why he needed to impose a 10 PM curfew on weeknights, with a midnight curfew on weekends. Saying nothing, I am sure I looked at him as though he had two heads.

Having no plans for that day, I did not venture out, but I did work the next day, Monday. I remember I had an excruciating headache the entire day and all I *really* wanted to do was to go home so that I could sleep; however, on the way home I realized this would be "giving in" to my newly imposed and entirely unreasonable curfew, and I was too innately a contrarian to allow for that.

I devised an alternate scenario; I showed up on my friend Michael's doorstep and asked if he would allow me to take a nap on his couch for a couple of hours, that I had a horrible headache and would explain when I woke up. He indulged my eccentricity and allowed me my nap.

I awoke a little before 10PM (*"Uh oh, a weeknight!"*), and Michael and I sat at the kitchen table and talked. This was a very common occurrence around this kitchen table; all our friends enjoyed the discourse and debates sitting at that table generated, and the wisdom garnered therein.

I explained my newfound constraints and why I needed to stay out past 10:00, even though I had been feeling under the weather; if I did not do this, I felt my parents would be out of control. And Michael, having a sympathetic ear to begin with, understood my dilemma.

So, we had coffee and chatted until after 10:30, and when the clock neared 11:00 I told him I could safely leave. Physically, I still felt horrible, and in all honesty would have preferred to have been home and in my own little bed, had the situation been different. However, two weeks before I left for college was, in my opinion, a ridiculous time to try to exercise constraint over me; either my parents trusted me, as they habitually illustrated they had throughout my life, or they did not.

I got home an hour "late" my first night of purgatory and immediately went to bed.

I never again heard a peep about curfew and two weeks later, after entirely ignoring my newfound limitations, left for college feeling as though I had somehow scored a point. But the bottom line was that my parents had not ever needed to worry about me or how I handled things; I felt that this had been proven out time and again in my life and leaving "the nest" for college did not change that, nor would limiting my movements immediately prior to leaving prevent their little nest from emptying.

That's my story, and I'm sticking to it!

The Early Morning Call

Every little girl has dreams of her proposal, and her wedding. I do not care how much anyone protests; it is ingrained into our genetics; it's just <u>there</u>.

Very few of us, however, realize how 'messy' life can be. We have this idealized version of adulthood, yet when we reach that magical age, or that magical event, or that magical place in life we dreamt of achieving...it just "isn't". It is not perfect, or it is not serene, or it does not solve our problems as we imagined; and we are disappointed.

Almost no one projects reality into their future. They project reality *as they want it to be, a*s I did.

In my early twenties, I met a man, David, and we started going out as friends as I was currently dating another. He was flirtatious, he was charming, he was engaging, he was funny, and generally, he was the life of the party. Unfortunately, I also believed him to be gay. But that was OK; I thought he would be perfect for my friend, Jimmy, and wanted to arrange a meeting.

I dragged Jimmy to the restaurant that David managed for an introduction. He agreed with my suspicion David was gay, but there was no spark between them. Oh, well. That did not stop me from hanging around with him, because he was quickly becoming one of my closest friends.

And then it happened. One night, he "put the moves" on me. I called a time out and asked him – point blank – if he was gay, because my assumption was that he was. I really wish I had understood his behavior better at that time, being absolutely appalled that I would even consider him to be gay. He was *adamant* that he was not gay and offended that I would think him to be so. I was a fan of Shakespeare at that time, and I would have been well-served to recall the idiom, "methinks thou dost protest too much" right about then, but I did not.

My parents raised me in a progressive suburb of Chicago. Granted, it was back in the 60s and 70s, but we still had open minds about such matters. So, I had a talk with myself and decided that you absolutely could not judge a book by its cover; and that even if he had some 'effeminate' qualities, if he tells me he is not gay, I was going to believe him.

I began seeing him in a new light, and I found that I was, indeed, also physically attracted to him, once my mental 'barrier' had been removed. So, we began dating. We were inseparable, for a while. From October of one year, until late April of the next, where one of us could be found outside of work, you could probably find the other.

He met my friends; I met his friends. I introduced him to gay bars (where my friends and I generally hung out); he introduced me to his hangouts. We even did the whole "meet the family" routine. Although, I do not believe he was any more taken with mine than I of his, there were very divergent reasons for that.

However, nearing the end of April, I became confused because I could feel him pulling away; I did not know why, but he was. Our relationship, up to this point very congenial and inclusive, became simultaneously rocky and passionate, and difficult to predict.

On the surface, everything seemed OK; but (you gals out there all know when this happens), "something was wrong", something felt "off", and he was not talking to me about it.

Of course, my first assumption was "another woman". I am not the type to stalk, I am not the jealous type, and I am not the sleuthing type. If circumstances presented themselves that this was the case, I would count myself lucky to find out prior to any commitment and simply walk away. It had happened in the past, of course, and probably would happen again. So, I just bided my time.

Soon I noticed that the calls were becoming less frequent, and the conversations, when they took place, stilted and tense. I realized that this was, indeed, the beginning of the end. As I said, not my first rodeo, so I knew what was coming; it was just a matter of time.

Then it came; he called to ask if I wanted my 'stuff' back. The ultimate, "thank-you-very-much-for-playing-now-be-on-your-way" card. OK. I had hoped for more with him, but apparently it was not meant to be.

In the meantime, although I was not initially ready to let go, while we played out this charade, I was mentally preparing myself for this very end. When it finally happened, it was more a relief. At last, suspicions confirmed (*I was not crazy!*) and I had a resolution.

I picked up my stuff and went on my merry way. Yes, I was depressed. Yes, I missed my best friend. Yes, for a while I was inconsolable. But I also knew I would get over all that; time and distance would heal me, there would be someone else, and I would be fine.

Spring melted into summer, and summer slipped into fall. I was emotionally 'back on track' and flirting around, but not dating anyone specific yet. And then it happened. At 3:40 AM, my phone rang. It was one of David's female friends, Karen. She confessed to me that he had been totally despondent since our breakup, and that they spent half of their time cruising past my house. She said she was tired of it, and had taken it upon herself to contact me, as they 'happened' to be in the neighborhood; she asked me point-blank how I felt about him.

At this point, while I was over the pain, I did still love him; I wanted to see him, and I wanted him to be OK. That's what I told her.

She said they were at the White Hen Pantry near my house, and she would continue to talk on the pay phone (to nobody, after I hung up), as that had been her ruse to keep him in the store while she placed this call. According to her, he had no idea with whom she was speaking. I told her I'd throw some clothes on and be there in a few 'with the boys' (at 3:40 in the morning, I took my Irish Setter, and my 120-pound Malamute/Pyrenees mix as protection, of course).

When I arrived, she was gabbing and laughing on the phone outside, as though she was speaking to someone; I wondered if she had indeed called someone after she hung up with me, she was that convincing!

I watched David wander around inside, eyeing the products, obviously bored, but probably taking nothing in; then he saw me. Our eyes locked, and everything around me froze, until he came outside. Karen ended her call, and discreetly slipped into the store.

We had an awkward conversation, but he did finally admit that he wanted to see me again; that he missed me more than he could have ever imagined, and he wanted to make a date, a special date, with me at Fountain Bleu that Saturday night. I accepted.

I went back home, my head and heart reeling, and I realized I was not as over him as I had wanted or imagined; he still had a firm hold on me.

That week seemed endless, and when Saturday came, I met him at his place. I did not know what to anticipate from the evening, and since the whole family thing had not gone well, my parents were just as happy that we were no longer together. I did not want to burst that bubble if things did not work out; if they did, they were going to be surprised, to say the least.

We went to the restaurant. I had never been there before, but as it was his favorite, I had certainly heard about it, and it was beautiful. Once conversation became more comfortable, he confessed he wanted to get back together. And he told me, while he was not 'officially' proposing, that was his intention.

I reminded him that our breakup had been, in part, because he never wanted to be a father, and that I could not envision life without children. His response was that he would rather live a life with a ton of children, if it included me, than live a life without me. Later in life, I would have seen this statement as the red flag it was, but I was still young and idealistic: I still believed that love conquered all!

See, ladies? In all the scenarios I had envisioned in my head as I was growing up about how this scene would play out, this situation had never emerged; but it still worked. We did eventually get back together, and we did eventually marry. It did not prove out to be that magical place I fantasized it would be in my youth; and it most certainly was not the marriage of my youthful dreams.

Sometimes, reality bites.

The Eerie Elevator Ride

I was getting divorced. I was not pleased with this prospect, or my life, and I felt as though I was losing my best friend. No, strike that. I *was* losing my best friend. We had been together, in one form or another, for the better part of a decade. So, looking forward to life without him was not even a concept to me; I was very afraid for what that life held. As a result, I worked a lot.

It was my outlet and considering we both still lived in the same house, my refuge. My 'light' workday was Sunday – I came in at 8AM and left around 3PM, with no lunch. The money was phenomenal, but I was just escaping, not allowing myself to feel. Because I knew that, right now, feeling was not something I could handle. So, I worked.

I worked downtown, and (especially after the Oklahoma bombing – thank you, Tim McVey) security became a real issue in all downtown office buildings. Elevators were locked off until you either showed security your badge or had swiped the same on an electronic plate; you all know the drill. You have been TSA-ed (now, a verb, thank-you-very-much); this was just the precursor.

Early one Saturday I arrived at my building. I worked on the 21st floor, and, technically, that should have been the only floor to which my security badge would allow access. But this morning, I went into the elevator, alone, as it was between 6:00 and 7:00 AM on a Saturday morning, scanned my keycard and pushed 21.

No beep. No halo of light shining around the 21st button that I pushed. The doors remained open.

I scanned my card again, and I pushed the button again. Nothing. Hmmm.

Then, unprompted, the doors closed; I scanned my keycard again, and pushed the 21st floor button. Success! The little halo light around 21 lit up, and the elevator began its ascent. Whew, that was close!

At the tenth floor, the elevator stopped. Although I was the only one in the elevator, I looked to see if 10 was pushed, also. Habit, I guess. Then the doors opened, and the light around 21 went out. I did not understand what was going on, but I decided I had had enough of this elevator, and I exited.

This floor was under construction; there were no lights on, and dawn was creeping in. Being a downtown building, 10 is not high in the scheme of things, so the surrounding buildings filtered out most available daylight. There was just enough light to make it feel eerie.

I crept forward, wondering how the elevator had not only stopped at 10, but opened the doors; there had to be someone here.

It felt like a lifetime before I was able to navigate to the stairwell. There was absolutely no way I was getting back into that elevator again; indeed, the gaping mouth of the offending elevator remained open in place as a creepy monument to my fear. I could not get away fast enough, but I was afraid for what I may find, and the darkness slowed my progress.

I reached the stairwell door: Ah, safety!

Except, it was dingy in the stairwell, too. But at this point, dingy beat creepy hands down!

So, I went down to the ninth floor and tried the door: locked! Then eight, then seven: all locked.

Great, no one knows I am here, they will find me locked in the stairwell in a month, having starved to death beating on a door: what an appropriate end to my life!

I finally made it to the first floor. Yay! Except the door was locked. *"Seriously?"* I thought. I pounded on the door and tried yelling, but these are fire-rated doors made of metal. There was no way anybody was going to hear me!

After assessing my situation, I realized I needed to continue downstairs and see where the stairwell leads. I presume, eventually, it will lead...somewhere?

I navigated down to sub-1: locked.

I descended to sub-2 and the door opened! Once again, I am in an unfamiliar place with no human aid to be seen; this is ridiculous! Now I am lost in the unfamiliar bowels of the building, with no obvious point of egress. *[Do you know how much damage I could have done, were I so inclined?]*

I tried to figure out how to get back up to the first floor when I spied an out-of-the-way staircase. This was not core building stuff, this seemed like more of a tenant build out, without security elements built into it. I prayed that it would lead me eventually to a door that would open.

And it did!

I was never so happy to see security in all my life! I approached the security desk intending to report my little escapade with the belief that I was performing a service to the building. Instead, they lectured me about compromising locked floors.

[Are you kidding me? Did you hear what I said?]

I slunk back to the elevator bank, having been made to feel like a pillager; and I still had to get upstairs. Sigh, my life!

The Elevator Ride

J t was Christmas!

My favorite time of the year!!! Traditionally, I launched my own personal Christmas in June when I began playing Christmas carols, and by August my room would be adorned with Christmas lights. Back then, that was the only holiday for which lights were used, and they were ceremoniously placed and removed each year.

I spent much of my time planning, plotting, and creating for my Christmas gifts – the whole season was amazing to me!

Mom decorated the whole house, and she made special once-a-year-only goodies. We generally teamed up to create quite an array of Christmas cookies to have in the house and to give as gifts. We each had our favorites and made sure they were plentiful. We were both in our own little heavens when Christmas season arrived.

But my father, not so much. Not that he did not like the season, he did. It was just that he did not do anything to display his enthusiasm. Or maybe my mother and I had so many bases covered between the two of us, we crowded him out. I do know that he hated shopping, and that his Christmas shopping trip was relegated to an annual excursion; my dad would take me out for me to help choose my mom's Christmas gift. This became 'tradition' between me and my dad. And of course, he procrastinated until December 24th, or thereabouts; no wonder he hated Christmas shopping!

One year, December 23rd rolled around, and my dad asked me if I wanted to go Christmas shopping for my mom, which of course I did! We ended up (surprise, surprise – as we always did) at Marshall Field's. For those of you reading who are neither from my vintage nor from my area, this was one of the higher-end stores in the area at that time. And quite popular at Christmas! The bonus was that they were also renowned for their fabulous Christmas themed window displays, back in the days when that was "allowed", so I looked forward to seeing those, also.

We got there and needed to go to the fourth floor for whatever it was we had decided to get her. We were the last two to enter the very crowded elevator, immediately prior to the doors closing, but there was room enough for the two of us. Being a gentleman, he held the door so that I could enter first. I got in and cozied into a corner. He waltzed in and the doors closed behind him. However, he remained standing in front of the doors with his back toward them.

Facing the other elevator riders created discomfort for them and made most of them feel anxious and awkward. This was creating tension in the air, and my dad surveyed the passengers, cleared his throat and said, "You're probably all wondering why I called this meeting."

Immediately, the tension was broken, and the atmosphere became festive again. There was a general rumble of laughter and a feeling of camaraderie between the elevator passengers.

I, however, was 13. Personally, I was praying that the elevator floor would open and swallow me before I died of shame and embarrassment; you cannot take parents anywhere!

The Encounter

I returned from college without finishing my curriculum; it would be hard to finish something you had never chosen. There were many reasons, but honestly, the predominant reason was that I just was not interested in scholastics anymore. I had become cynical about the entirety of the educational system, and I was in a hurry to begin my life, not to prolong my teen years.

I secured a full-time job. And I was busy when my friends came home from college for the summer, or on break, because I was working now. I was a 'grown up'. I was making money. I was, frankly, making rather good money, in comparison to what they had.

But then something happened. They graduated. They came home and collected their offers. They had options. Now, it seemed, I did not. I was now paying the price for my impatience to become a grown up. This was something I had to come to terms with, although the upside was that now they were working full time also, and did not have summers off, or breaks anymore. We all worked pretty much the same hours, so we saw more of each other.

One of my friends, Jackie, had accepted a position that mandated a lot of travel. She would fly here and there and, generally, I was her personal taxi service. This was back when you could enter the airport to both pick up and drop off people, obviously pre-9-11, and even pre–Oklahoma City.

I spent a lot of time picking her up, or dropping her off, and I enjoyed the driving part as well as spending the time with her, either waiting for her plane or meeting her at the gate. Of course, picking her up meant a visit to the luggage carousel, too. That part, I did not like. I found it annoying to wait for the luggage gods to disgorge luggage out of the bowels of the terminal. During that time, I would step to the side and wait a distance away, leaving her to curse the luggage gods by herself.

One such occasion, as I was standing there, I noticed another woman standing near me. She caught my eye, and then she nodded to me and gave me this look. I did not know what she was saying, but it seemed that she was trying to communicate something in it. I smiled at her, looked away, and contemplated.

She did seem familiar, and it was almost as though she knew we knew each other and was acknowledging that fact. I was trying hard to place her, when Jackie came up to me to tell me she had retrieved her luggage and we could go. I turned to the woman, smiled and said, "Bye. Have a good evening."

As I we were driving home, Jackie was prattling on about her trip, but I do not know what she was talking about; my mind was fully consumed with that woman in the airport. She did nod with familiarity, and I did recognize her; I just needed to place her. Suddenly, I got it!

I slammed my hand on the steering wheel, and exclaimed, "Rhea Perlman! That woman was Rhea Perlman! And I will BET she was waiting for Danny DeVito to get their luggage! Unbelievable!"

Jackie looked at me as though I was off my rocker. I never explained; at that point, there was little reason to do so. I was simply happy to finally place the face.

The Family

Family dynamics for us was quite unique. However, having said that, I believe that every family could probably make that same statement.

For most of my young life, I viewed my parents as creatures to teach. For some reason, having been raised in a more urban setting and, frankly, having a seemingly more adventuresome spirit than anyone else in my family, I really felt that I was, in a way, raising my parents. And that this was my role in their lives. And I have to say, I did a great job!

Family Portrait

They were raised in the same little town, went to the same school, in the same rural area of the state. I, on the other hand, felt quite "cosmopolitan". I was raised in an affluent town, although I did not realize it at the time, as we were the 'poor relative' of the neighboring town with which we shared our high school. We were located right outside of the city limits, immediately adjacent to one of the diciest neighborhoods in the city. So, I *knew* how to handle myself! [*Oh, if only I could go back to those brazen days!*]

My brother, I cannot explain. I have always loved him and wanted a relationship with him, but for some reason we could never connect. He is a loner, yes, and certainly has his own way about him, but we could never really communicate with each other on a human level. That holds to this day, and it weighs heavily on my heart.

I had a conversation once with a friend who was trying to fix me up with one of his friends. Late in the conversation, he threw in the question, "Do you know anything about red heads?" "My brother is a red head", I responded.

To which he said, "Oh, then you know."

"Know what?" I asked.

He explained, "Well, I am not exactly sure if they are walking a few steps *in front of us*, or a few steps *behind us*, but they sure as heck aren't walking *with* us!"

I thought about how aptly that described my brother. I had never put that together with his being a red head, but it did make sense for him. Whether or not that is a universal truth, I do not know. But it was apropos for him.

Still, I feel a profound sadness in knowing that the one person to whom I am most closely related is the one person with whom I will probably never have a relationship. Enough said on that topic.

Mom was a 'stay-at-home' mom which, at that time, meant she was a 'normal mom'; when I grew up, that was standard. Moms stayed at home and took care of the house and the kids; Dads went to work.

That was the deal. Occasionally there was the couple who flip-flopped: dad stayed home and took care of the kids and mom worked, but that was rare. On the even rarer occasions where there was a kid from a single-parent home, we felt bad for them, because that generally meant a tragedy had struck the family and one or the other parent had passed away. I remember only two people from my childhood who came from 'divorced' homes; it was an anomaly, and taboo, at that time.

At lunch, we were excused from school to go home to eat. We all lived within walking distance, and had an hour to go home, eat, and return. My favorite days were the days I came into the house and smelled Kentucky Fried Chicken (pre "KFC"); that was a special treat! That meant my mom had been out and did not have time to make my lunch, but I did not care. That was also back when they only had original recipe, but they did not call it 'original' because that was the only option. No grilled, either. Pure, unadulterated fried chicken. *YUMMERS!*

This was also about the time of the appearance of "Swanson's TV Dinners," another lunch favorite of mine. I only liked the kind with the brownie; I did not care what the entrée/vegetable selection was, but I needed that brownie to make it complete. Sometimes, mom would cook one of those for me for lunch: another treat!

Dad was a teacher at the high school I attended. He had a three-block walk to work and was home by dinnertime. Mom had dinner ready at 5:00, and we ate. We sat down at the dinner table and ate together. If one of us was absent, we knew ahead of time, or they were in bed, sick. Other than that, this was just how families spent dinner time; no calendar juggling, no standing-at-the-counter-wolfing-down-food-so-I-can-get-out-of-the-house type thing, we just sat, and ate together. And we talked. It was nice.

Dad always liked to play

I was close to my dad as I grew up; we had a special bond. I believe every father and daughter does, but nowadays, so few get to experience it. He was my pal. I could tell him my secrets and be (relatively) assured he would not rat me out to mom. It was a comfortable relationship, and we enjoyed our time together.

Being goofy with dad

My mom's and my relationship took more time for me to understand. I was aware she thought the sun rose and set on her son; being a 'daddy's girl', I understood that. At least, intellectually. In my heart, I must admit, it hurt. Because I also knew that my dad was fair – very fair. Even though I was always 'daddy's little girl', I also knew that when push came to shove, his rewards and punishments would entail equal justice, which meant that sometimes I got the brunt of it. This also meant that I was on an uneven keel with my brother, and always at the disadvantage; he always had mom on his side, and dad was bipartisan (maybe I am beginning to understand the rift with my brother?).

And my mother could frustrate me by doing too much. I know this sounds strange, but for a kid with a strong independent streak like me to have things done for them is frustrating. She would do things like ask me if I want to re-decorate my room. [*Why? It is perfect as it is.*] But when I would start thinking about it and get excited about it – BAM! – Mom would strike! I came home for lunch, and she showed me the curtains and bedspread she picked out for my new bedroom, just to show me, mind you. I did not have to keep them if I did not like them.

So, what am I going to say: they are horrible, I hate them, and I especially hate the fact that you did not include me in choosing them?

"They're fine, mom. I like them." She re-did my room. And so it went. I would get excited about a project, only for her to 'help' me out of my enthusiasm. That was our relationship. Not bad, basically good, but tending to be annoying.

It took many years, but it finally happened.

My first marriage took place when I was 25. My parents did not exactly love my choice in partners, but then again, they did not have to live with him. Unfortunately, neither my mom nor my husband could seem to let bygones be bygones. So, I always felt that I was in the position of having to choose between my 'family' and my husband; and please note how they were two separate things. That was how it always felt, unfortunately. More so on my husband's side, later, than my parents', but still, a choice.

After four years of marriage, it became clear to me that we, as a couple, were not going to succeed. It was both our faults; I am not going to get into details here, because it just is not important. Suffice it to say that, after this wound had festered now for more than five years, I had to admit to my parents, my mom in particular, that I had not chosen well; that I had failed, and that she had been right.

I was not looking forward to this, but eventually of course, it was going to become obvious, so I had to do it.

I took my vows very seriously when I married. And the thought of becoming a 'divorcee' was almost untenable to me. There was shame for me in this designation. Self-inflicted or not, that is how I felt. I had made a mistake – publicly – and now I had to admit it – publicly; that was how I saw it.

When it came down to the wire, and I had to pack my things and move them out of the house, my mother was there to help me. I was so torn up about the breakup – my husband had been my best friend for the better part of ten years, between dating, courtship, engagement, and marriage – and now we were to go our separate ways. Every time I stood up, I became nauseous and had to run to the bathroom. This happened the entire time we were packing. My mom plugged away, packed, organized, straightened things up, did all the mom things that she was there to do.

She comforted me while I was lying on the bed crying. She rubbed my back and tried to soothe me. I felt like I was standing on a tiny little throw rug, and that somebody was not only pulling it, but the whole floor along with the entire world out from under me. I was in a deep abyss, falling, and searching for a lifeline.

On the last day my mom was there to help, all had been packed and carted away. As she was leaving, we said a perfunctory goodbye, and she began to walk away. She stopped, hesitated, then turned around and walked back to me. She said, "I don't know how you feel, I've never been through this myself. But I want you to know that your dad and I love you, and we are here for you; and if you need anything, please just let us know."

My mom had the biggest "I told you so" in the world coming; but instead, she chose, at that very second, to become my best friend. And one that I sorely needed at that point!

Thank you for always being there for me, Mom. I love you!

The Family Dog

I was home from college, with my "family". My two dogs, an Irish Setter (McCabe), an Alaskan Malamute (Temba), and my orange tabby cat (Squirt). I was moving back home to live with my human family, until I decided what I wanted to do with my life. Or at least until I got a job!

For the duration, the four of us were camping out in my old digs (i.e., my old bedroom). There were no issues with me, the cat or the Irish Setter, but the Malamute was proving to be a challenge.

When I first met and purchased her, she lived in the country, on a farm, in a pen with her mom, dad and sister, amidst a cornfield with a small outbuilding as their home. While they were in their pen, they were comfortable and sociable, and there were no red flags that I could see. But, removing her from her environment after I purchased her was an entirely different story. She was not aggressive; she was just clueless as to how to interact, although I got the feeling that she wanted to do so. They bred the puppies, but had apparently not socialized them, to anything.

From the way she behaved, I believe their 6-ish-year-old daughter was the only person in the family who actually paid attention to the dogs. Temba carried that love for children, specifically little girls about that age, her entire life. She never did really understand what to do with them, she just knew she loved them. She would stand with her nose buried in their chest, happily wagging her tail. To a 6-year-old girl, this was quite the intimidation! She loved them; she just could not properly convey that feeling.

And so it was with everything!

From the moment I brought her home, everything was foreign to her; the leash, the collar, the car, the car ride (she never did get over car sickness), the stairs, the people surrounding her in her new home, being inside, the TV, the other pets. Everything, to her, was new and unfamiliar, and I believe at least to a certain extent she was shell shocked. This poor baby had nothing, *nothing*, around her that was either familiar or a comfort.

She was on overload and, for all practical purposes, was in a catatonic state for about three full days. We had to carry her down into the basement, where we fed the dogs, set her in front of the food and leave so that she would eat. Sitting in the living room, she would stay in whatever position you put her; she was afraid to move. The only time I saw her relax was when she was around our dogs, an Irish Setter and a German Shepherd, with the human counterparts remaining far from the play. She was familiar with dogs, so she was comfortable with them.

Temba, next to her two new 'trainers', McCabe & Lucky

I taught my dogs to walk with me off leash, and to respond to voice and hand commands. It worked well for me and had the side benefit of having nobody on the street dare to approach me. People tend to stay away from large, unleashed dogs, especially German Shepherds!

But until she was trained, Temba needed to be on a leash. Getting her on one, though, was a conundrum. I put it on her collar, and as soon as I did, she planted her feet – all four of them – in opposition to me and the direction I wanted her to walk. And if I changed course, so did her feet. Whatever I did, she was not going to budge; she was not willing to surrender one inch of territory.

I coaxed, I pulled, I bribed and finally I begged; nothing seemed to matter. She was absolutely, dead set against walking cooperatively on a leash. I was about to give up when I had an epiphany. She loved our dogs and would follow them anywhere. I called McCabe to my side, and took the leash off Temba, showed it to her, and put it on McCabe's collar. Who, frankly, could not care less whether he was on a lead. I then signaled for him to begin heeling, and she decided to tag along, because he was there. I hand signaled for him to sit, which he did. I took the leash off his collar, showed it to her, and put it on hers. Then I asked McCabe to heel again; he did, and she tagged along, simply because he was there. I spent a lot of time transferring the leash from one to the other, making sure she saw each and every time I did so.

By the end of the day, she was walking fine, by herself, on the lead!

I used him more and more often to communicate with her, as she trusted him much more than people. I figured I was going to have to continue speaking to her through him until she gained trust in humans; once I did break through to her, she became *my dog* and resented me leaving her. At all. For _any_ reason. For _any_ amount of time, effectively, she put a leash *on me!*

There were other barriers she had that I needed to work on, but we were now in a better place, and I had a foundation on which to work with her.

This was about the time I was questioning why I was in school. I did not believe in higher education, anymore, at least, the higher education that I was experiencing at my college, and I could not think of a vocation I wished to pursue. So, I decided to get the show on the road, so to speak, and begin "my life". I moved home, with "the kids" to look for work and figure out what I was going to do for the rest of my life.

McCabe was fine, my parents always did love him, and he was never any trouble; the cat also acclimated beautifully to their house; Temba, on the other hand, was a handful because of her background, and the fact that everything you did with her needed forethought in approach. And most people are not used to doing that with their dogs. But, because she did not speak "human", those who interacted with her needed to be fluent in "dog", which most people are not, and you really had to want to bridge that gap.

For instance, when Temba sat down in front of you and stared at you, she wanted to be pet. This is uncomfortable for most people, because she did not give tail wags or any other indication that this was a friendly encounter; she just stared at you and expected that you would understand that she wanted affection.

Even though I tried – awfully hard – to get my mom to understand this, it apparently did not click. She was always more of a cat person, anyway, and her reaction to Temba's stare was to stare back, effectively challenging Temba every time Temba was asking her for affection.

After repeated rebuffs, the result was that Temba eventually learned to steer clear of all things 'mom'. So, when I was gone from the house, she snuck in and out of the house using the dog door, and when she was inside, she would roost in my room, on my bed, where there was a level of comfort for her, and she used that as her sanctuary. She did not hang out with the rest of the family, as did McCabe. She was either outside or in my room, waiting for me to come home.

I genuinely believe that as a direct result of the stare-downs that she and my mother had, each one resulting in her tucking her tail and slinking away, she became resentful toward our family dog, who was pretty much my mom's.

The family dog was a 14-year-old small long-haired mutt, white with a couple of black spots, named Rags. She had cataracts, effectively blinding her, and was at least hard of hearing, if not entirely deaf. She had survived two strokes of which we knew, maybe had suffered more when we were not around. I had advocated for a while, especially after watching her last stroke, for my parents to put her down and not let her suffer through another. But mom would not hear of it.

Our family dog, Rags

Bottom line, though, was that Temba associated Rags with my mother. And Temba tended to be more than a little vengeful.

My mother called me one day, hysterically crying. She yelled at me that my dog had killed her dog. I instructed her to immediately take

Rags to the vet, that I would pay any vet bills incurred. To which she responded, "You don't understand – there's not enough of her to take to the vet. Rags is dead!" and she hung up.

I was new on the job, but I figured that this qualified as a family emergency, and I should probably get home to find out firsthand what happened.

By the time I arrived, my dad had cleaned up as much of the mess as he could, and just by assessing the residual, I think I was glad that I was not first on scene. What I saw was bad enough!

First, Temba was locked outside, and I was told in no uncertain terms that she was not welcomed to stay anymore. It was surreal to see her greeting me, wagging her tail and so happy I was home while her mouth, chest and feet were covered in blood. Rags' blood.

I walked past her and up to my room, where I had been told it had happened.

My room had white wall-to-wall carpeting, white floral wallpaper, and a white drop ceiling. There was an area in my carpeting, much too large to be called 'a spot', that was a deep crimson red, and absolutely saturated with blood. When I looked around, I realized that there was not one wall of my 12' x 14' room that did not have blood splatter. And yes, it was even on the ceiling.

What in the world had Temba done? My heart was broken for both my childhood companion, and my mother, who had found her.

I do not doubt that what my mother said was true – that by the time she found her, there was no hope for survival. I could not believe what I saw, and I could not abide the stench anymore. It was heavy, and damp, and metallic.

I believe that, when I left the house that morning, Temba did her usual routine – walked me to the car, spent some time relaxing outside where she felt comfortable, then went inside to her sanctuary, to nap and await my return.

At some point, I imagine Rags wandered into my room, as she was wont to do. Temba, protecting the only turf she had in the house, probably gave all the 'normal' warning signs – jumped down from the bed, growled and snapped warnings at Rags; unfortunately, being deaf and blind, I am not sure Rags ever knew.

And so, Temba acted upon her territorial instinct. It was very macabre, and nothing that I could fix. I just needed to get her out of the house and into her next home, wherever that would be, and hope that she could begin again without me.

I never imagined that welcoming my dogs into their home would end like this for my parents or our family dog; I had no idea how to make this up to them, or what to do for them in their grief. This was a challenge that we somehow would need to navigate together.

My parents were surprisingly resilient, and eventually even welcomed one of Temba's puppies into their home. I determined that when I grew up, I wanted to be like my parents. Either one, it did not matter; they were both excellent role models.

The Family Visit

Incorporating Bronson into our family was initially very scary for me; after all, I was the one who had brought his mother into our house and let us just say it did not end so well. I was shocked that my parents would not only entertain the idea, but they embraced it.

He was the "pick of the litter" between my Malamute, Temba, and my ex's Pyrenees, Blue Boy. This puppy looked like a little polar bear and was as adorable! A friend of mine had told me that he was in the market for a dog, a large dog, having had enough of his wife's sheltie. When he heard about these pups, he asked about them, and I told him the mother is 75 lbs. and the father is 120; there was no way this would be a small dog! He told me he very much wanted him! He kept saying, "The bigger, the better!" I thought I had found a suitable fit, and that everybody would be happy.

When the time was right, I took the trip to Temba's new home, and brought back her little white polar bear pup. So far, the only one she had ever had who was pure white. He rode the entire way back on my lap, and I fell in love with him. I kept reminding myself that I was taking him to give to one of my friends, and that was all. I took him to his new 'Daddy', who sang praises about him. The first thing he did was name him Bronson, because of his eventual size; he wanted a strong, 'man's dog.'

Polar bear cub or puppy? Baby Bronson

Initially, Bronson stories were prevalent at my workplace (that is how I knew my friend), but eventually the frequency of stories dropped. I just assumed that the novelty of having a puppy had worn off, and that was the cause. Unfortunately, four months down the line (Bronson was now six months old), he told me that he wanted to return Bronson; he told me that was growing way too large. At six months, he was 60 pounds.

Uh, yeah. That is what I told you!

So, he came back, and for a solid week, I really was trying to find him a new home. But then I decided he had a home; my parents seemed to love him, and they were not holding any grudge against him, so I started playing with the idea of keeping him, along with my Setter.

Unfortunately, I did not convey this idea to my parents, who were still under the impression that I wanted to find him a new home. My cousin, Teddy, and his family came to visit, and they fell in love with Bronson. They talked it over with my parents, who still were not aware I had designs on keeping him, and they agreed to take Bronson home with them. They were even happy with his name, which would have been Bronson Johnson!

When I got home, my dad came to deliver the good news to me he had found Bronson a new home!

My heart sank, and I guess my dad saw that on my face. He asked what the problem was, and I could not even talk, I just cried. Not wailing, just looking at him with tears streaming down my face, trying hard to breathe. My dad caught on immediately, and asked if I still wanted to find him a home, and I just shook my head no. He handled it from there; I never said a word to my cousin about it, but they left without Bronson Johnson.

So, I had another dog! I was overjoyed, as was my dad. My dad had this huge soft spot in his heart for Bronson, so it worked out well all around.

Although Bronson had another canine friend, McCabe (my Setter), McCabe was rather aloof when it came to other animals; I firmly believe that he was under the impression that if he paid no heed to other animals, they simply did not exist. And he did not like sharing me with anything or anyone, so that was the attitude he adopted, which left Bronson open for a friendship with my cat, Snapper.

Snapper at batting practice

The two worked beautifully together. They had a system whereby the cat would climb up to the high shelves on which my mother placed her baked goods in order to keep them away from Bronson. Snapper would push them onto the ground, and Bronson would take over from there.

My mother would come home to pieces of aluminum foil decorating her back yard, and the broken casserole dish would be shattered on the kitchen floor; she did not have to guess what had happened (although I think it did take her a little while to realize that the two were co-conspirators).

Bronson and Snapper devised games together. They played hide-and-seek, and Snapper was convinced that if she hid her head under the couch, she was hidden from Bronson; she was so convincing that Bronson believed her, or at least pretended that he did. If Snapper's head was hidden, Bronson "could not see" her and would continue his search for her. I believe they kept each other company most of the day.

One day my mom called up to me in my room to tell me that she thought something was wrong with Snapper. I really did not think there was a problem, but I came down to check it out. She was literally dragging her front right leg as she tried to walk.

My dad and I took her to the vet and discovered that her leg had been shattered. An injury like this, he said, is deliberate – she got hit with a baseball bat or something; he did not believe this to be an accident. He gave little hope of repairing the leg, he would have to go in and literally wrap a wire around the broken bones to get the shards to mend together; and even with that, there was no hope of a proper repair, he said the leg would probably always give her trouble.

He suggested, and we opted to comply, that we put her down, so we came home empty-handed.

Bronson was confused. He walked around the house for a week looking in all the hiding places in which Snapper had hidden; under the ottoman, under the couch, under the chair, in her favorite bed: no Snapper.

Eventually, I think he decided to expand the search, and the fourth time our 75-year-old neighbor retrieved him from wandering the streets and placed him on our front porch, I decided it would be better to find him another home, one where he would like to stay and maybe had a little more land attached, rather than to allow a 120-pound dog to wander our suburb at will. I knew he would not cause trouble, at least not intentionally, but he was a little large to set loose on the suburban population.

So, we found him a farm home; one where there was plenty of room to roam, and he had a Doberman buddy with which to play. From the onset, I understood that those two really hit it off.

He had been at his new home for about six months, and I had gotten married in the interim. My husband and I purchased a home, and we were busy working on it. So many changes, and it left little time to visit my parents. I think my dad was feeling nostalgic, and he asked if there was any way we could visit Bronson.

I told him I did not see why not and got the information about the new owner from my ex, Jim, the one who had placed him on the farm to begin with.

My parents and I chose a date, the following Saturday, and I asked Jim to relay the information regarding our visit to Bronson's new owners. Saturday rolled around, and we piled in the car for our three-hour one-way trip to see our big baby, Bronson. I even had his puppy pictures – the ones where he looked just like a polar bear cub – and was planning to present them to his new owners.

We got near the area, and somehow got lost. Not a big problem as this was in my ex's hometown, so we stopped by his parents' home to say hi and to get directions. Barb, his mom, was startled when we told her what we were doing there. She said, "But Bronson is dead."

And told us how he had gotten hit by his new owner's truck as he chased it. Ouch!

She said she was surprised that Jim would give us such misdirection, but apparently, he had recently had a string of bad luck with his dogs. His Great Dane had fallen ill, and he took him to the vet. The vet kept him overnight, declared him well and released him; the Dane died the following night. Blue Boy, Bronson's father, was found dead in a creek bed after a flash flood at about the same time. That was followed by the news of Bronson. She was guessing that the news of Bronson probably just did not sink in, and that was why he gave us the information he did.

We chatted for a little while and caught up with her and the family, then piled back into the car.

My dad started the car, turned around to me and asked, "Any more dead dogs you want to travel three hours to not see?" At least we got quality family time out of it, and a chance to catch up with Barb!

The Fire Department

I committed to it. I told my parents that I would mow their lawn while they were on their extended European tour. Of course, it was the least I could do, since I had run off, gotten married and left my two dogs for them to house. I had to be there daily, anyway, to take care of the dogs, and I lived in the same city. So really it was no big deal, and it just made sense.

I have never been good at getting any gas motor to start; I just do not have the arm strength for the rip cord. However much I tried to ignore it, a week into their vacation, I noticed that the lawn really needed to be mowed. Darn it! I was hoping I could let it slide until they came back, but that was not going to happen.

I went about picking up the yard (*did I mention the two large dogs?*) and then I got the mower out of the garage. And tried and tried and tried to get it started. Boy, this was difficult! I kept at it for what seemed like forever. I pulled and tugged and tugged and pulled until finally – something happened.

Except, it was not the mower starting: there were flames, springing up from somewhere around the motor. And I had no clue what to do! I knew better than to try to douse a gasoline fire with water, but then...what?

I herded 'the boys' (my dogs) into the garage and ran into the house to call the fire department. I told them that I had a potential explosion on my hands, and gave them my parents' address, noting for them to come down the alley to the back, where the mower was.

Then I kept watch over the back yard and my firebomb, dogs tucked safely away in the garage.

Eventually the fire department showed up. Since I had asked that they come the back way, it was not until they showed up that I remembered we kept the back gate locked because one of our young neighbors thought it was entertaining to see the dogs run loose; I now had to navigate past my 'firebomb' to allow them access into the yard. In retrospect, probably not my best idea, but the mower had not exploded yet, so maybe I was safe.

I dodged the (now defunct) fire on the mower, and let them in. They did a cursory inspection of the mower, borne more out of formality than any real concern, and asked again what had happened. I told them, and even showed them where the fire had been (which, of course, was now out).

Most of them just exchanged indulgent glances, and then wandered back to the truck. One of them stayed behind to let me know that I should probably tell my parents to get a new mower, then he likewise moved on.

I was able eventually to successfully start the mower and mowed their lawn. Thankfully for both me and the fire department, it was just the one fire.

I do not remember ever relaying any message to my parents regarding their mower; but I do know that all my mowers since have been cordless . . . *and electric!*

The Gift

*H*eredity is a curious thing. There are some things that are explicable, eye color, hair color and texture, stature, body type. All of these are characteristics traceable back to one or another parent or lineage. I remember learning about fruit flies in high school Bio; it is a simple concept.

And then, there are things, the intangibles, that seemingly have no genetic basis for inheritance, such as the talent to be the only one at the table in a restaurant with the ability to find foreign objects in his food. Both my brother and I have somehow inherited that talent from my dad. The irony is that if we were both sitting at the same table as my dad, we were safe, because my dad trumped us every time and he would find the 'object'. So, I ask you: how is this an inherited trait?

My dad was a teacher, and one February attended an out-of-town teacher's conference with about a dozen of his colleagues. Because it was February, back in the olden days when we celebrated both Washington's and Lincoln's birthdays rather than the generic "President's Day," the special for the week was cherry pie. Everybody at the table ordered a piece of cherry pie for dessert.

When dessert arrived, my dad said, pointing to his piece of pie, "Wait! I will bet anyone at this table $50 that this is the piece of pie with the pit in it. Further, I will double that amount if someone wants to exchange his or her piece with mine that *THAT* will be the piece with the pit in it." Nobody took him up on his offer, and on his second bite, he spit out the pit; no one else had one.

And this, somehow, we inherited from my dad.

Tangential to this gift is the ability to stand in the line that, immediately after the person in front of us cashes out, the cashier will be called to break, or there will be a change of shifts, or they must do a register accounting at that precise moment, prior to our purchase. Sometimes they even walk away from their drawer, with no explanation, no promise to be back momentarily, no acknowledgment of us in any form, just *POOF* gone!

Recently, my daughter and I traveled to Canada by car, and I chose the shortest line in customs. The line on each side of us was running about four cars through to our one; however, much like my dad's cherry pie example, I knew that, should I dare to change lanes, THAT will be the line that slows down. So generally, I do not bother. We waited, and waited...and then, finally, we were next in line.

The car in front of us was dismissed, the door to our agent's booth opened, and the border agent walked out of the little shelter, strolled over to the next agent's booth, and began a conversation with him.

Really? We were the next car in line, but there were others, quite a few, behind us. Leaving us all wondering what we were supposed to do. It did not seem to bother her that we were all waiting for them to finish their conversation or whatever. Eventually, she came back, with no explanation, of course. I guess that was just her break.

Another talent my dad seems to have bestowed is what he called the "No thanks, I've been waited on already" look. The look that chases away salespeople from our general vicinity. They assume, or want to, that we have already been helped; even if we are standing in their line, awaiting their service.

The most egregious example of this gift came while taking a trip to my parents' house with my daughter, about four years old at the time, and we traveled by tollway. Halfway to their house was a tollway Oasis with a McDonald's, so we would stop for a bathroom break, and a treat if she was hungry. This time, we arrived just behind two buses letting their riders out for lunch. Yay.

There were about ten lines, and each line had a minimum of 15 people in them. So, I settled in for the duration. As I got closer, I was amazed at how quickly my line was moving: will miracles never cease?

And then, "The Look" must have struck. I *finally* got to the front of the line, and the cashier leaned over the counter to peer behind me and asked the man standing in line BEHIND me if she could help him.

"*EXCUSE ME???????* *What about me?*" I asked. To which she looked at me, startled and confused, and replied, "I thought you had been waited on."

I said, "I'm standing in YOUR line – have <u>you</u> waited on me?" She shook her head no. "Then I guess I haven't been waited on now, have I?" That one took the cake!

And this is hereditary...*how?* Can anybody explain this to me?

The Gift[2]

I was independent. I had just announced to my parents that after two grueling years of college, I was leaving school. I was scheduled to get married in the middle of the next semester, and my fiancé lived an hour away. Somehow, I thought it might be problematic if I were in school.

But apparently, since I was leaving school, my parents expected me to be self-sufficient. Wow! I did not see that one coming!

My mom asked how I was going to pay for my apartment, and of course I told her I would get a job. Well, I showed her. I got one that very day, I was an opener at Arby's. I enjoyed it; there were many people to talk to, and my material needs were few. This job kept me sufficiently funded for my lifestyle. But I got so bored that I went out and got a second job, a waitressing job. I had never been a waitress in my life, but I figured I was a college dropout – it could not be that hard!

And it was not. Really,

And, between the two (even with the little bit I was making), because I did not have the time to go out and spend money, it just kept accruing. It was a simple life, a life I loved. Just me and the dogs. And my pile of money, growing larger and larger.

The only thing that I missed was a car, which I really did not need (I walked everywhere, I always did), but with two large dogs to feed it would have been helpful to have a car to haul their food from the grocery.

As the jobs progressed, and I met more and more people, I met one in particular of whom I was fond. A young manager at Arby's, John, and we had hit it off. As it turned out, that was problematic for both my impending nuptials, as well as my fiancé. But that is another story...

We got to know each other well, but our relationship had to remain in the closet; for not only was I engaged, but he was one of my supervisors, so it was *verboten!* Of course, I have always bucked the rules!

One of the things that he suggested was that I borrow his car to pick up dog food. This was a Godsend, as I had to buy in bulk to save money (I did not make all that much) and one trip to the store in a car would save me two or three trips walking, dedicated to purchasing their food.

I took him up on it, and LOVED it – he drove a Bronco, which was a relatively new model at that time. I was an SUV fan from way back!

I went to the store and made my purchase, threw in a few extra errands because I loved driving the car, and headed home. I was coming up to the stop light at Goodwin, which was red for me, and I put my foot on the brake. Nothing happened. Immediately assuming that I had mixed up the gas pedal and the brake, I tried to move my foot to the left and found...*NOTHING?!*

I could not stop! My foot HAD been on the brake. Oh, no! What should I do? I was approaching the red light, with another traffic light yet to go, and then a circular drive to access my house; my brain was on overdrive!

Because I have always loved driving but have occasionally been bored while doing so, I had practiced different scenarios of driving. One of the things I practiced for no apparent reason was braking a car using the emergency brakes only, for which I was now relived I had done. Putting the brake pedal all the way to the floor did nothing, so I used the emergency brake to slow the car down and eventually got home using that technique. I unloaded the car, then called John to ask why he had not told me there were problems with the brakes when I took the car.

He was dumbfounded; he said there was no problem with the brakes and wanted to know what I was talking about. At his insistence that there was nothing wrong with his car, he talked me into getting into the car and driving it back to him. OK, it is your car!

I crept back to return his car, almost not engaging the accelerator for fear of not being able to stop. Eventually, I got there, and he immediately took his car for a test drive.

He was gone an uncomfortably long time, but eventually returned. He claimed that he had absolutely no problem with the brakes, and that he had no clue what I was talking about.

"*What? How could that be?*" I thought to myself.

But I figured I had done my due diligence informing him of the issue; what he did with that information now was up to him. In the meantime, I would continue to walk to the grocery store.

A couple of days later, I came into work, and John asked me about specifics on the incident. What exactly happened, what was I doing, how it happened, etc.

I ran through the scenario a couple more times for him. During this discussion, I was taking off my coat and putting it on a hanger to hang on the coatrack, and expounding on how, if something was going to go wrong, it would happen while I was in the vicinity.

I had just finished this statement as I put my hanger on the coatrack, and it collapsed in front of me. Totally. At my feet.

I looked at him and said, "See? What'd I tell you?" and walked away.

This is my life in a nutshell, and I have accepted that. Sometimes, it can even be amusing!

The Gift from Santa

I was a daddy's girl, and I followed him around like a little puppy dog, especially on those days when he was working in his self-created "shop" on the back porch. His creations fascinated me, and I wanted to absorb everything I could. He really did not have a "shop" on the porch; we lived in a three-story walk-up Greystone apartment building, but his tools and a workbench had made their way to the back porch, and this is where he spent a lot of his time when he was home. As a result, this is where I spent a lot of my time.

One night my daughter-radar sensed that he was out on the porch "creating" so I trotted out to see what he was doing. He was working on a pegboard box, as far as I could tell. I really did not care what he was working on, I just wanted to be with him. He showed me the box, which had a handle at the top and a hinged door on the front, and told me that he was making a surprise for my mom for Christmas: a knitting box. I was too young to realize the impracticality of the explanation, but then again, my only goal was to spend time with my daddy.

Months later, on Christmas Eve, my brother and I were looking forward with anticipation to the following morning, Christmas Day!

Christmas was always an "event" at our house; mom would get us all dressed up in our best clothes, and we would come into the living room only to be blinded by the movie lights attached to my mom's movie camera. Half the time, we could not see where we were walking for the blinding lights, and the resultant movies were of the two of us scrunching up our faces and shading our eyes from their offense. Regardless, once the camera was off and our eyes adjusted, we were able to see what Santa left!

But this Christmas morning, after the lights were gone, I was frozen in place. Santa had forgotten me! I was trying hard to think of what I had done to make him forget me, but here I was looking at the bounty he left, and there was nothing for me. My brother had his fire truck, my mom had her knitting box; try as I might, I could find no third present.

I stood there trying hard not to cry; bravely suppressing the tears that wanted to stream down my face while trying to face the fact that my Christmas would be present-less from Santa. I had been judged, and it was now public; the world knew I had not been good that year.

That is when my dad stepped in; he pointed to the knitting box and told me it was mine. I stared him down, contorting my face in my best little girl, "HUSH" face in order to get him to be quiet; that was mom's knitting box, and I was not going to take it from her, regardless of my humiliation.

He walked over to it, unhooked the fastener to the hinged door and showed me the Barbie kitchen contained inside, replete with appliances, wallpaper, and a kitchen table! I was ecstatic; Santa had not forgotten me at all!

I will be totally honest here and say that I was not thrilled with this gift; I was not really a "Barbie" kind of girl. Although I had one, she just was not something to which I devoted a lot of time. But the fact that Santa had not forgotten me; that was priceless!

It took me well into my adult years to realize that, somehow, even that experience did not shake my belief in Santa Claus; I never questioned his existence. The power of belief is extraordinary!

The Good Dream Shampoo

To say I had an active imagination while I was growing up would be an understatement. The images I had in my head could spring to life at any moment and jump at me; the wallpaper in my bedroom although floral, seemingly had springs in their bouquets and would jump out at me as I tried to sleep; I saw tigers jumping through my (third story) bedroom window to stalk me. This probably added to my natural disinclination to take naps.

Putting me to bed at night was a chore for my parents; for those imaginings of the afternoon became true terrors at night. I had monsters under my bed, and I had to jump from the hallway threshold into my bed, or the monster would grab my ankles and pull me under; I had monsters in my closet whose capabilities were yet unknown to me; and the flowers of the afternoon would jump at me, although sometimes they became Coo-Coo clocks, springing at me only to retreat once again. I was up and down again and again, "trying" to go to sleep.

I could not spend too long in my bedroom without something terrorizing me, and ultimately my solution was to crawl into bed with my parents. However, I think my dad was unhappy with my solution.

One day, he came home with "Halo: The Good Dream Shampoo". Although I was unfamiliar with this campaign slogan (because it was non-existent), my dad said it was so, therefore I believed. He had me take a bath and wash my hair with this 'good dream shampoo' before I went to bed, and he told me that would end all the nightmares.

That night, as the tigers jumped through my window and the coo-coo clocks sprang at me, I was too scared to get out of bed for fear of the under-the-bed monster grabbing my ankles; and I endured, for my father. I did not want him to be disappointed with his "good dream" shampoo, although I knew it to be false. It took me a while, but eventually the practice of just 'enduring' and not running to my parents' bed took hold.

Years later, in my adulthood, my dad asked if the good dream shampoo really worked. I told him that no, it did not stop the nightmares, but I did not want to disappoint him.

"Then it worked," he said.

And I guess, from his perspective, it did!

The Great Train Ride

J had a love/hate relationship with one of my best friends growing up, Janice. Well, maybe not so much a love/hate relationship as much as she was exceedingly competitive (more so than I ever realized) and occasionally I would compete back. Neither of us liked losing, so there was a lot of ego and pride mixed into the friendship.

We spent most weekends hanging out. We usually spent Saturday together, had a sleepover at one or the other's house, and I would accompany her to Sunday school the next morning. It worked well all around, generally.

Together, we thought of some creative 'projects' to keep us occupied, such as pouring ketchup all over ourselves and lying in our street's gutter to see how many cars would stop to help us (*answer: none*). We did not, however, factor into the equation that it was July and exceptionally hot; we were lying still, or trying to, with sticky sweet ooze on us. Obviously, keeping still while volunteering as fly bait did not work out well and we quickly tired of it. But when we put our heads together and schemed, we could come up with some doozies!

One Saturday morning we were bored with the routine, so we pooled our resources, walked to the Metra train station, and purchased two one-way tickets to the end of the line. At that time, it was

Geneva, although the line has since expanded. We did not think things through, and I do not believe it occurred to either one of us that we may be in trouble trying to return, as we had just spent most of our money; we were young.

On Saturdays, all trains are local, so all stops are made. We pulled into Villa Park, and the 7-11 was right at the train station. We decided to hop off and get some snacks (we did have a few cents leftover from our ticket purchases). As we had not really formulated a plan and we had not anticipated being away from home, we were both hungry. We could afford some sort of chips, and some canned bean dip, which I had never had. While it was filling, I cannot say it was my favorite.

We knew the train came through again in an hour after we had disembarked, so when it came near to arrival time, we dutifully waited at the station ready to hop on board. If either of us had been regular commuters, we probably could have figured out that the trains only opened the doors on one side; and we were not on that side. The train stopped, and the doors opened on the other side of the tracks. As hard as we pounded on the doors, they remained closed to us. Lesson learned, and now we had another hour to await the next train.

And we were still hungry! This time, we did not even have change left, so we tried not to think about it. After serving our hour of penance, when the train arrived, we made sure we were on the correct side.

We boarded the train and remained on until we reached the end of the line. But now that we had reached our goal, it became obvious to us that we did not have a game plan; so, what were we to do?

The area seemed vaguely familiar to me, and I thought this may be near where my mom's cousin, Judy, lived. Well, not here exactly, but close. Ever since I was little, I have enjoyed a wonderful sense of direction and can generally find places, even if I had only been there once. This area did seem familiar, so I told Janice to follow me: we were going to make a social call!

We headed off in the direction I was almost positive we needed to head. Maybe. After walking quite a distance (probably only about a half hour, but it seems longer when you are not entirely certain where you are heading), Janice was looking for some assurance from me, which I could not genuinely give, but I could fake well. I mean, after all, I told her I knew where we were; if I needed to walk the circumference of this entire earth, I was not about to backtrack and admit I was wrong; not in front of her!

So, we walked, and walked and walked. At least the scenery was beautiful, as we were following a wooded trail next to the river. She kept looking at me, wanting to ask if we were still headed in the right direction; I plodded confidently on, ignoring her tacit inquiry, knowing/hoping we were on track.

Soon we arrived at Main Street, and I knew we were in St. Charles. Hooray! I now knew we were on the right street! Inside, I was doing a happy dance because I would not have to admit to her that I was wrong; until I realized each way up and down the street looked the same, both familiar, and now I did not know which way to turn. *Hmmm...*

I told her to head to the left; no reason, it just seemed correct to me, although I did not tell her that, I told her I knew for sure. And we walked. And walked. And walked. When we hit a shopping center I recognized, I knew we were on the right track! But then again, there was a General Mills factory across the street from the shopping center, and I did not recognize that; I did not recognize that at all!

Since I had successfully navigated us this far, I thought it would be appropriate for us to call Judy, to "make sure she was home" and knew we would be visiting; in other words, I wanted her to confirm we were heading the right direction!

We placed a collect call to her and happened to catch her at home; she would be delighted to have some company, and I told her where we were. She said we were on the right track, to just keep heading in the same direction.

See? I knew where we were all along!

So, we walked. And walked. And walked. We were about a mile away from their house, and I saw their station wagon heading down the road, straight toward us. Our rescue squad was arriving!

In the car, after she picked us up, she said that she was waiting for us to appear after our phone call. Then, as time passed, she began thinking: "They aren't old enough to drive: how did they get out here?" That was when she got in the car to find us walking. When we got to her house, she called my mom to let her know where we were. I daresay, my mother was neither perturbed, nor surprised.

We spent the rest day in their pool (they had suits for us to borrow) and played/swam in their ponds. Then she drove us to the last train back and even paid our way home, God bless her!

I often wonder if it even occurs to the younger generation today to attempt a journey such as this; or, if they did, how well that news would be received by their parents. What joy and adventure we have sacrificed as a society; this is one of the most cherished memories of my childhood! RIP.

The Grocery Store

In one of the many iterations of my life, I lived in a rural area of Missouri, seven miles outside of town, in the woods off a gravel road. Although the town was small, we did have our own grocery and hardware stores, as well as a restaurant. It was really the first time in my life that I ever seriously thought about cooking. I was raised baking every sweet imaginable, but cooking? That was never even a fleeting thought running through my mind.

At least, until I went to the town's one and only restaurant. Everything – *absolutely everything* – came smothered in gravy. I have never been a fan of gravy to begin with, so this restaurant was not an instant favorite of mine; as a matter of fact, I think that may have been my only excursion there. All I know for sure is that I was absolutely *dying* for a twice-baked potato, which they did not have.

I was already feeling quite sorry for myself and for the mess I had made of my life. I felt that I had married the wrong man, and for the wrong reasons; I was removed from "home", my family and my friends; and then to find myself in such a location where they did not even eat civilized items such as twice-baked potatoes, well, that pushed me over the top! Oh, I was having quite the pity party; at the age of thirty-one, my life, in my opinion, was over! I was alone in the country, with unemployment at 24%, located literally one hour away from anything at all familiar to me.

It was a couple of days later, as I was bemoaning my fate that I now lived in such a God-forsaken place that had never even heard of twice baked potatoes, that the thought occurred to me that I could make them myself! I am not sure why that was an epiphany, but it was. And once that thought crossed my mind, I realized that the possibilities were endless! I could have lasagna, and twice baked potatoes, and rice pilaf, and shrimp de jonghe again! Maybe life as I knew it was *not* over!

I was thrilled at this prospect, and began straightaway perusing my cookbooks (yes, I had them – I just never looked at anything outside of the dessert sections). Wow! So many recipes, so little time! It was time to go on my first real trip to explore the grocery store, and I had my little list of ingredients I needed to make lasagna in my hot little hands.

When I opened the door to all possibilities, not just the baking section, I noticed and then marveled at the items in that grocery! I had never seen pig's feet, tripe (*yikes!*), tongue, liver, and kidney; everything imaginable was in that butcher case, as well as the rest of the aisles. I wondered that anybody could use 5-gallon buckets of lard. Lard! The only thing I had ever seen come in 5-gallon buckets was joint compound – needing or buying that much lard was beyond my comprehension! (*Although I found out later that is what makes for very flaky pie crusts: who knew?*)

I was raised in a neighborhood heavily influenced by Italian culture, and my friend's mother was Sicilian. I used to tease her all the time, and when I visited, I would open the fridge and tell her that I would like some ricotta (intentionally mispronounced) "ra-KOTT-ta" cheese, inflecting the word in my most pronounced South Side Chicago accent, knowing that she would cringe and say, "ri-GO-tah, ri-GO-tah", rolling the "r", and emphasizing the Italian pronunciation with her hands. So, I became used to 'her' pronunciation of the cheese.

I ventured over to where I thought the ricotta should be. Hmmm. . . not here. I had all my other little lasagna ingredients together in my cart; I just needed that one last piece of the puzzle, and a rather important piece, at that! Now, if I were ricotta, where would I hide?

I must have looked very confused because someone asked if they could help me find something. "Yes, please," I said, "I'm looking for ri-GO-tah cheese."

Blank stare.

"I mean, ra-KOTT-a cheese." Blink, blink. "Let me call the manager; maybe he can help you."

[Yes, I DID just land my spaceship in your parking lot, thank-you-very-much!]

So, she paged the Manager, and I told him what I needed. He said, "Perhaps if you tell me what it is, and what it's used for, I could help you find it...?"

"It's like a dry cottage cheese, and I've already looked near that. It's the cheese used in lasagna." He took me over to – guess where – the dairy section! And, right next to the cottage cheese, I saw one tiny, little section that had containers of, right again, ri-KOTT-ta cheese!

I learned two things from this experience: First, to do a more thorough search the first time, prior to involving anybody; and secondly, more importantly, the only constraints you have are the ones you place on yourself.

Lessons learned!

The Gym Class

J was a "TK". Anyone who was a "TK", or a "PK" knows what that means. I was a teacher's kid, and I had to toe the line; I had to be "an example". Yes, it had built in perks, but sometimes as a teen, you had to maneuver through minefields. And most TKs in the school knew the other TKs; at least, we knew who they were, if not personally. PKs were Preacher's kids; they have a congruently similar, yet altogether higher expectation. One with which I could empathize.

When we first moved into our house, I aligned myself with another TK who lived two doors down from us (the "original" Ann in our neighborhood, and the reason I was not allowed to keep my name). Ultimately, I became better friends with her younger sister, Janice. I was two years Ann's junior, but only one year Janice's senior; and honestly, we were a better match. However, by the time I reached high school, I had parted ways from both.

So, I was a TK, and one of my best friends, Jackie, had Ann's father for class; Chemistry, to be exact. Pronounced *KEE-mo-stry* by "Farmer George", Ann's father, the chemistry teacher.

Jackie would regale me with her adventures and frustrations during our gym class, Archery, which was scheduled immediately after her KEE-mo-stry class. She would tell me horror stories of conversations with Farmer George (he had that nickname because of his 'southern' accent), and it was universally known amongst the students, at least in my experience.

She had difficulty grasping chemistry and would go in early for extra help. The conversations with him were always circular, and they went like this:

> Jackie: "I need some help with the homework, I didn't understand it."
> Farmer George: "Did ya DO yer homework?"
> Jackie: "Yes."
> Farmer George: "Then ya under-STAND yer homework."
> Jackie: "But I don't understand it."
> Farmer George: "Then ya din't DO yer homework."
> Jackie: "But I did."
> Farmer George: "Then ya under-STAND."

I think you get the picture.

One day, after a particularly grueling KEE-mo-stry class, Jackie came in, guns a-blazing about "Farmer George". Our archery teacher told us that day about the importance of having a focal point in your bull's eye; that day, for her, that focal point became Farmer George. And she made no bones about it! I think there was not a soul in that class who did not know her focal point that day, and why.

And then, it happened.

I got that prickly sensation down my spine, telling me that something was happening behind me of which I should be aware. I turned and looked.

I had totally forgotten that Farmer George's daughter, and my former friend, was in this archery class!

And I somehow suspect that she, also, knew who the 'focal point' was; that is, if the look I was getting was any indication, which I am sure it was. I smiled at her and shrugged.

Oops! Sometimes, there is just no recovering from a bad situation; all you can do is hold your head high and press on. Good life lesson!

The Ice Cream Bar

We all have them: first loves. Mostly, they are a warm, nostalgic place to reminisce. But, then again, you could have mine.

I met my first "real" love through a friend, who had a crush on him (and half of his soccer team). She invited me to go with her to a party the team was attending. But, let me back track just a little.

None of my little 'clique' of six friends had been invited to the prom our junior year, and we were hosting a 'consolation' prom so that we at least had something to do that night, lame as it may be. Liz and I came up with the concept and we had fun running with ideas and planning a formal dinner dance for the six of us.

We created bids to purchase for our alternative prom, with the musical theme of "Love Hurts", by Nazareth. The backdrop had a silhouette of a man and woman dancing, with the man, of course, stabbing the woman in the back. We compiled a long list of heartrending tunes to play, so that we could really have a great time at our pity party.

We generated a menu for our six-course meal, and Liz's mother had agreed to purchase dinner wine for us to consume with the meal. We all went out and got 'prom' dresses and headed over for an evening of jaundiced festivity.

At about 10 PM, another friend, Mary Anne, showed up to drag me away to a party. Frankly, by that time I was tiring of both hosting and eating, so I was happy to take a break between the endless courses. I know I helped to plan the meal, but I think we may have been overly enthusiastic. (*What were we thinking? We were still cooking Baked Alaska at 2:30 in the morning! I am not sure any of us was interested in eating at that time, although I will admit that the whole idea of baking ice cream fascinated me!*)

I freed myself temporarily of hostess duties and ran out to the other party with a couple friends; this is where I met 'him': Scott, my first love. From the beginning, we were captivated by each other; however, I did have a party I was co-hosting, and I needed to return. I arrived back in time to pull the Baked Alaska from the oven, and both Liz and I sighed in relief – it was over!

After that weekend, Scott and I spent every waking moment together. I snuck out of the house at night to meet him; we would go out for hours, just talking and driving. He even tried to teach me how to drive his family's VW van (a manual shift), which was a dismal failure. I am still not sure how much permanent damage I did to that car.

I was in heaven. I had finally found my one true love: the love of my life and deemed myself so lucky to have found my soul mate so early in life.

For six weeks.

Then, he went on vacation with his family. They had a vacation spot they went to every summer, and this was the week. I felt OK about it, though, as I really got along well with his family, and he gave me his pet mice to take care of while he was gone. How much more could I have asked?

But when he came back, he did not call, not even for his mice.

And when he did finally call, I could feel the difference. Something was wrong, and we were no longer in the same 'space' we had been. He had pulled back, and I did not understand why.

During the time we were together, I became good friends with his sister, Jane, one year my junior. We had much in common, and I enjoyed spending time with her outside of my time with him. So, I reached out to her when I felt things had gone south, and she confirmed there was 'another woman'. Someone who was not even in high school. She was *a graduate*, and an older, 'more experienced' woman. She was twenty, and even had her own car.

I was devastated. He was my one true love. How could he treat me like this, after all we had been to each other? I mean, it had been six whole weeks, for goodness' sake.

After I reconciled myself to the fact that we were, indeed, 'over' (and I was able to finally get rid of his smelly mice), I was grateful for the fact that his sister and I had met. We became dear friends and remained so for decades after that.

Bottom line, even after our breakup, I continued to hang around the house. I didn't understand his new relationship, as they always took her little sister on 'dates' with them; that seemed rather odd to me.

And then there were the physical differences between us. I was 5-9", 132 pounds, a Swede through and through, with long straight blonde hair. My clothing preferences tended to padded shoulders, cinched waists with skirts in the style of the 40s. A-line, with calf-length hems.

These two (I must lump them together, as the two sisters were never apart) were about 5'-2, and I am sure each out-weighed me. And, having Sicilian heritage, let us just leave it at they were not blonde. But they did have long hair. They preferred to wear slacks, and I had a hard time not confusing them with fireplugs. Oh, I am sorry; I did not mean to write that.

One night Janie and I were out with another friend, Anna, and the three of us ended up at Jane's house. Her mom was going to bake something, but the walnuts she purchased needed to be shelled and chopped. So, we were sitting at the kitchen table, shelling and chopping walnuts for her mom.

Then, *they* came in: the trio. They raided the freezer, and each grabbed an ice cream bar.

I decided it was probably time for me to go home anyway, as it was nearing 1:00 AM, and I said as much. The three of us agreed to call it a night, so we were heading outside for Jane to drive us home.

To this day, I am not sure who said what, but one of the sisters said to the other, "I wonder why she wears skirts all the time?" To which the other responded, "She probably can't find pants that fit."

I was at the back door, the last of us three heading out. I stopped in my tracks, turned around, smiled and said, "That's kind of like the pot calling the kettle black, isn't it?" And turned around to leave.

I heard footsteps quickly running toward me. By this time, I was in the back yard; she grabbed me by the shoulder, whipped me around, and I saw her arm winding up, ready to punch. I steeled myself for the blow, but instead I got a cold lump of – something – on my face. Then I realized what she had done: she had 'slapped' me in the face with her ice cream bar!

Which struck me as extraordinarily hysterical, and I burst out laughing, infuriating her even further. I was laughing so hard; I was having a hard time keeping hold of her hands that now *were* trying to punch me. Janie was behind her, yelling at her stop, which she would not do. Jane grabbed her by the hair, twisted a handful of it and jerked her backwards to separate us.

Except I was holding on to her hands, and what happened in effect was that she pulled her down and, being attached to her, I fell on top of her. I was still laughing; but now, even harder.

She realized then the position she was in, and she stopped trying to hit me, at which point I let go. After we both righted ourselves, she immediately whipped around to Jane and yelled, "Why don't you like me?"

That sobered me up, so I chimed in, "Hey, if your issues are with her why am I the one standing here with ice cream on my face?" That was right before I started laughing again.

Then she turned to me and accused me of throwing eggs at her car as she drove down the street. I told her I had better things to do than to stand on street corners holding eggs while waiting for her to pass in her car. She asked me, "If it wasn't you, then who was it?" (*Please, do not __ever__ extend me an open invitation, because I __will__ accept.*) I told her that I imagined there were *plenty* of people would like to do just that.

We got nothing resolved that night. Suffice it to say, the gauntlet had been thrown down, and I was not going to let the call go unanswered. There will be more of her later.

In the meantime, I saw that little Cissy-boy Scott was watching the whole thing safely through the window. I was glad that I was able to see this side of him. Suddenly, I did not miss him quite so much; with that one action he tremendously aided me in getting over him.

Thank you, Scott!

The Instructor

When I was in second grade, my teacher was really impressed with my artistic 'talent'. I put that word in quotes, as I have never been as impressed as she with my abilities. She was so impressed that she contacted my parents and offered to send me to the local art school, and I mean she offered to pay for the lessons. She was a spinstress, maybe even by that time, an 'old maid', and had no children of her own. She was quite fond of me, and vice versa. Although my parents did not take her up on the offer, they decided that if she was that adamant about my talent, they should investigate enrolling me in art lessons themselves.

I was not aware, until later in life, that this offer had existed. All I knew was that I was suddenly thrust into this quasi-adult world of art lessons, where there were people of all ages, and I was most definitely the youngest. Initially, I was quite excited!

The first day of class, the instructor spoke for a while, and showed us samples of what we would be learning throughout his class. Then he gave us a verbal list of materials we would need to get. Being in second grade, I could not yet write, let alone take down a list of art materials necessary for my class. I tried diligently to remember every item he listed.

One of the only things I did remember him distinctly saying was "Pencils". I told my mom I needed colored pencils. So, we marched out directly after the class, and I chose a stunning set of pencils from our local art supply store; they were the most beautiful set of colored pencils I had ever seen!

I was so excited to parade in the next Saturday morning, proudly displaying my pencils. I was sure everybody in class would be envious of my new colored pencil set!

And then it happened.

The art instructor descended upon me, picked up my beautiful pencils, and asked me, "What are these?" I told him they were my new set of pencils that he said we needed. And he replied, "Pen*TELS*, I said you need Pen*TELS*, not pencils!"

And with that one sentence, he broke my heart.

I never did like the class after that, but since my parents seemed as though they wanted me attend, I never said anything, other than telling them I needed to go back to the art store to return my pencils and purchase penTELS.

I lost interest in "formal" art instruction that day, vowing that any creative endeavor ventured from thereon would be on my own terms.

I did not realize at that time, but this was a presage of things to come concerning my disappointment with our educational system, but that is another subject!

The Journey

My daughter, Savanna, called me at work in a panic. Our dog, Ginger, would not stop throwing up, and she was scared. Realizing there was nothing I could do from work, I told her I would deal with it when I got home. By the time I did get home, Savanna was holding Ginger 'hostage' in the bathtub just so that she did not have to repeatedly wash the floor/dog anymore; just rinse and drain. *"Rather clever on her part,"* I thought.

Ginger was doing better by the time I arrived, so I told Savanna we would watch her and see what happened. Within a half hour, she was back at it, so we hauled her off to the vet. After some x-rays and bloodwork, it was determined that she had pancreatitis, and she would need an altered diet, among other things. We had adopted Ginger as an adult, and by this time we had owned her for ten years. I had been without any dog for seventeen years prior to adopting her, so she was the recipient of seventeen years of pet depravation, and was indulged quite liberally by me; apparently, much to her detriment.

Along with the pancreatitis, which was already an eventual death sentence for her, the X-rays disclosed a growth about the size of my fist in her stomach. Since we were already dealing with one life-threatening illness, we decided not to pursue the cause of that growth; her life was going to change significantly enough as it was. Whatever else came, we would handle as it emerged.

We were able to enjoy her for the better part of another year. Eventually, it was obvious she was struggling, and that it was time to think about scheduling her final vet appointment. I cannot remember the reason, but one morning I realized that it needed to be scheduled sooner rather than later.

We had an appointment scheduled for our 14-year-old male cat that Friday, two days away, for a dental cleaning assessment. I told Savanna that I would try to schedule Ginger near that time so that we could take them together; but that if they had no openings, I would need to usurp her appointment and take Ginger.

The vet clinic understood the situation and accommodated both. They took Ginger in back to 'equip' her with an IV, and to begin her general sedative. They brought her back to us and took Cinnamon in back for testing and assessment while we said our good-byes to Ginger. We were to let them know when we were ready.

When that time came, they gave her the final dose of sedative inconspicuously, allowing us our privacy as much as possible. They monitored her and told us when she was gone. I held her paws for a while longer, just because I did not want to let her go, even though there was nothing we could have done for her anyway.

Farewell, Ginger. We'll miss you!

After a few more minutes, there was a knock on the door. When the vet came in, I knew there was more trouble; tears welled in her eyes, and she began the conversation with, "I hate to tell you this on today of all days, but Cinnamon is not a candidate for a dental cleaning." She continued to say that she believed he had lung cancer that had metastasized into his liver, he was in stage two renal failure, and he also had pancreatitis.

Although I love all animals, I am more of a dog person than a cat person; my daughter leans towards cats, and the two cats we had were hers. In an emotionally charged situation already, she took this news exceptionally hard; we came home with one less family member, and one more death sentence.

When we got inside our apartment, I told her that I needed some time to stare at a blank wall for a while; she was welcome to join me, but I wanted no talking, no TV, no radio, *nothing*. She wanted to be with me, so we ended up taking a nap together.

When I awoke, I was feeling better, or at least more human, so I got up and opened the flowers that some friends at work had sent me for Ginger. They were gorgeous, and I woke Savanna to show her. She also was feeling better, so we decided to put in a DVD of Dick Van Dyke; he is always comfort-food for the brain.

We sat down and started watching the show, both of us quiet as we absorbed the day's events. About ten minutes into the first episode, my phone rang; it was my brother and he asked if "the home" had called me. "No," I said, "Why, what's up?"

"Dad's gone."

I began laughing (my way of dealing with extreme stress), and I could tell that my brother was offended. I said "No, you don't understand. This is just the perfect end to a perfect day." I told him about the rest of our day, and I think he better understood my reaction. I got off the phone to relay the message to Savanna, but she had already gleaned the gist of our conversation.

I un-paused Dick Van Dyke, more to have background noise than anything else at that point.

Mulling everything over, it soon occurred to me that my dad and Ginger had been good buddies in life; how appropriate that they were traveling buddies in death. It gave me an odd comfort to know that she was already there, waiting for him, and they could cross that bridge together. I know they were happy to see each other.

Dad's empty bench

The Last Cigarette

No, I was not quitting. I just needed to run to the store to get more. The only cigarette I had left was, believe it or not, my 'lucky' cigarette. Now, you may ask "Isn't the term 'lucky cigarette' an oxymoron of sorts?" But the ritual went like this: upon opening each pack of cigarettes, I would take one, turn it upside down as I made a wish, and replace it in the pack. That was supposed to be the last cigarette smoked from that pack, and in theory, my wish would come true.

I did not believe it for one moment as I had waited over two years for that to happen; I did it more in the vein of tradition, or ritual. But I did like the 'ritual', and so I continued.

Before I went to the store, I stopped by my friend Jane's house to see if she wanted to accompany me. I had just that day come home from my first year of college and wanted to touch base with her. While I was in the house, one of the guys I had been dating when I left for school, John, stopped by. *Her* house.

And, from the reception he got, this was obviously not the first time he had, although when he saw me in the house, he tried to give me some song and dance about how he had been driving around and saw my car, so then he decided to stop in to say 'hi'.

Yeah, right.

When her older sister came out from the private family area and started razzing him, I knew this was obviously a relationship they had cultivated and enjoyed over time, and it confirmed for me that it was most definitely not a unique situation for him to 'stop by' Jane's house.

I need to backtrack a bit and admit that I was aware our 'relationship', if you could call it that, had been faltering for a while. I did not want it to, that was just the reality. And I did not know how to stop it from doing so, especially long-distance. Apparently, I now realized, that was also due in part to the existence of another woman, my friend Jane, being in the picture.

I am not dumb, and two plus two will always equal four, common core math aside.

I knew we had issues in the relationship, I knew even when I left for school that our relationship was quite lop-sided stemming from me. But knowing that did not stop the feelings I had for him, nor the sting that came from, in my opinion, their betrayal. Not only by him, but more so by her. They only knew each other through me, and neither one, apparently respected me enough to believe that it was any of my business to know that they were dating.

I found it easier to forgive him, as we barely had a relationship; Jane, I had known for years. She was one of my closest confidantes, specifically regarding my feelings toward John, and my acknowledgment that I was aware how one-sided it was. In my opinion, to not disclose her feelings or their mutual feelings to me during one of my admissions to her that I knew something was wrong was nearly unforgivable; that was the part that stung.

I went outside to cool down. Her friend, Anna, who was visiting, accompanied me outside. I asked her point blank how long this had been going on, and she said, "Oh, I think they're just friends." I skewed an eyebrow at her, and I think she realized I did not believe her; she quickly slunk back into the house.

Then he appeared, probably to attempt damage control.

When I saw John, I became agitated, and I already felt foolish; I wanted to have something to do with my hands, so I pulled out my ciggies. I took one out, and as per usual, he tried to stop me. I informed him that he certainly had no right to have an opinion on <u>anything</u> that I did. Not now, and not ever again.

To prove that point, I lit my cigarette. You know, the "good luck" one. The one that was backward in the pack.

I lit the filter. Of the last cigarette I had.

He looked at me and said with a smile, "I tried to warn you."

The Laundry Chute

J had a friend in grade school, Janice, and we were attached at the hip, most times anyway. It was curious that we wanted to spend so much time together, because we could be incredibly competitive with each other. But, whatever the case, we were a duo. We were the first to poke fun of each other, too!

My dad liked to work on the house and make what he considered to be upgrades. Quite often, they were upgrades that would not be found in other homes, as he had this unique ability to combine "energy saving" measures (*what can I say—it was the 70s*) with convenience, and the compulsion to utilize every "wasted space" in the house toward *a purpose.*

Take the front hall closet, for instance. He bought a refrigerator light button and installed it in the doorframe so that no one ever had to turn on or off the closet light: if the door was closed, the light was off; if the door was open, the light was on. To this day, I have never seen another house with that feature.

Janice liked to come over and test this theory. She could spend hours opening and closing the closet door, just to ensure the light was always on or off, as appropriate. I personally did not find the concept all that riveting, and I never pointed out to her she could test this same theory on her refrigerator at home.

Another gadget my dad installed was to put a "driver's button" on his La-Z-Boy chair, which was simply a hard-wired "mute" button running from the TV so that he could mute the commercials without having to get up from his chair. (*Both my father and my brother spent a lot of time at Radio Shack!*) And if you happened to be sitting in the "driver's seat" you <u>had</u> to mute the ads, or you had to abdicate the spot. House rules.

My parents owned an old Victorian house, which originally had an interior front and back stairwell. My dad felt that was redundant and decided to remove one of them; the one in back that ran between my room and my brother's. He wanted to use that space to enlarge our closets on the second floor, while enabling him to increase the size of the kitchen below by three feet.

Although I understood that I would be getting more closet space, I loved my current corner closet. It spanned the entire height of my room and had a substantial shelf about 1-1/2 feet from the ceiling. When I was not feeling well, I would climb up there to take a nap. It was totally dark, and nobody ever found find me there; it was a perfect place to hide, and it seemingly had healing powers, as I always awoke refreshed.

The other place I liked to sit and ponder was in the stairwell that was being removed. There was a window at the landing below and was a nice perch just to sit in the quiet, stare out the window, and think. I was going to lose both of my 'spots'; but nobody asked me my thoughts on either matter.

After the staircase had been removed, and closets built out, my dad realized that there was enough room to install a heat duct at the baseboard in the second-floor hallway to run straight down to the basement and into a laundry basket; this would serve as our new laundry chute. Although mourning the loss of my stairs, the laundry chute was kind of a neat idea; I liked it!

And apparently, so did Janice.

The first time she came upstairs after its inception, but before it was finished, she noticed this new hole in the wall. For whatever reason, her first instinct was to stick her head into the hole to see where it led. She got her head in, but because it was not yet finished or framed out, her ears apparently impeded her from extracting her head, without pain.

By the time I realized she was in a panic and yelling at me to get my dad, I was rolling on the floor, laughing; I could not believe she had gotten her head stuck in our new laundry chute! I told her I was going to get my dad, but I made a detour first. My dad was sitting in his chair as I ran past, but I was on a much more important mission.

I had to run to the basement, to wave at her and laugh. Ha! I could tell that she was SOOOOOOOO angry with me, but hey, it was worth it!

After I had my fill of teasing her, I ran to get my father to help. I could tell that he did not really comprehend what I was saying when I told him that she was stuck in our laundry chute until he went upstairs and saw the rest of her protruding from the wall. Looking back now, I have to wonder how he accomplished the extraction; but at that time, I was still too busy laughing to realize how confounded he must have been, and I cannot remember the solution he contrived to free her. All I know is that I had a good laugh at her expense, and she was no longer stuck in our laundry chute.

All in all, it had been a good day!

The Little Boy's Pain

I knew something was wrong; there was something very, very wrong. My mom was transfixed by the TV in a way I had never seen, although in 1963, that was not an unusual state by anybody's standards. After all, TV was still relatively new.

It was something else. It was what was *on* the TV that was engrossing her that was new. People were crying, almost inconsolable, and that seemed to be the sudden and predominant theme on the TV, no matter the channel. There were words I had never heard, "assassination" was one, and "Dallas" another. I kept seeing the same thing on TV: a car, a convertible, kind of neat, actually, traveling down a street.

And then, something happened. The man fell, his wife jumped, and then seemed really upset. And the people on TV were all upset. And then it would happen again. And then some people on the TV would cry, and I heard more than one person speaking on the TV whose voice choked up with emotion.

This happened for what seemed to me to be days, and days.

And then the scene on the TV changed. There was a grassy field, with a large crowd, and rows of chairs set up. There were speeches, and there was gunfire. The military shot their rifles into the air, while in full dress uniform.

My four-year-old mind had formulated a general idea as to what had happened, but I did not know exactly; I did not fully understand.

Until I saw him. I saw the little boy, in a little short suit, saluting a coffin. Then it dawned on me, and I understood. And I felt so profoundly sad; my young heart broke for this little boy. This poor little boy, whose father was never coming home again, who even I understood was probably too young to realize his loss.

That is how I remember John-John; and this will always be my memory of JFK's assassination.

The Misunderstanding

*A*s parents, I think we can all remember some of the goofy little things our kids did as they were growing up. We all have fond memories of a special way they pronounced things, a particular way they phrased things, or perhaps we just remember the indomitable spirit of our little ones.

But sometimes, we can remember those roles in our own lives. I remember when I was very young, when my brother was able to begin school, but I was still too young to attend myself; I resented his absence and was jealous that I could not go; life was so unfair! Not only had school taken my brother from me, but a lot of my friends, as well. I got bored during the day; I missed having him and my other friends around to follow.

I could not understand why I was excluded from this special "school club". The first week he began school, my mother tried to console me by taking me to see Mary Poppins – in the movie theater, three times. I did not realize until much later in life what a labor of love that must have been for her, and what a tremendously long movie it was!

To add insult to injury, I was still expected to take naps; I always hated naps. As a result, I have been watching *As the World Turns* since the early 60s. My mother would escort me to my room and put me down for my nap right before it began. I would stay put for two minutes, maybe, before I got myself out of bed, pressed myself against the dining room wall and sidled right up to the partial wall dividing the living room from the dining room. And I would sit on my side of the partition watching the show, as my mother sat on her side watching.

And I knew when it was time to get myself back into bed, so that my mother could come 'get me up' from my 'nap'. It worked well for both of us, for the most part.

One day, I was not at all tired, and it was a beautiful day. Instead of putting me in my room for my nap, my mother just instructed me to go take my nap. Hmmm. I did not feel like it, so instead of going to my room, I marched past my bedroom, straight through the house and out the back door to spend some quality time outside.

Once downstairs, I felt so free! I walked around the back yard. I thought about all the kids I knew who were in school, or home taking naps, as I should be. There was nobody outside to spend time with me. I became lonely, and bored.

Then it hit me: I needed to figure out a way to sneak back into the house before mom realized I was gone.

I thought, and thought, and thought. And why I thought I could not go right back in the way I came out is beyond me, but for some reason, that was not an option that popped into my head. I guess, because I had snuck *out* of the house, I somehow deemed it appropriate to sneak back *into* the house.

Now, how do I do that?

I had an idea; I would sneak in the front door (you know, the entrance closest to where my mom was sitting–makes perfect sense, right?). I walked into the apartment's entryway and tested the doorknob. Uh, oh, I had not thought of that; it was locked.

While I pondered over what I should do next, I heard something; something that sounded suspiciously like a mother, an angry mother, coming quickly down the front stairs, and right at me.

Think fast!

She opened the door, and just exploded on me about how she had sent me to take my nap, and how I was missing when she went to check on me and (honestly) all I heard was "Blah, blah, blah" because I was trying to figure out how to get out of this one.

When I realized she had stopped talking and was apparently waiting for a response, I had an inspiration. I looked up at her and said, "I'm sorry, mommy. We must have had a misunderstanding."

I marched past her and up to my room.

I am sure, as I was walking up the stairs, I heard a muffled laugh coming from her general direction. All I know for sure is that I never heard about it again.

The Name

We began our "permanent" life (where my dad had found what we later knew to be his permanent position, career-wise) in a Greystone apartment building. People who live in urban areas are familiar with this term; some may not be, but it is an apartment building built from gray stone with two upper floors, and generally has a garden apartment in the basement. In our case (and I do not know if this is typical) the first floor was divided into two smaller units, with the second story a 3-BR unit, which was our apartment.

This apartment was my sanctuary and comfort from when I was nine months old until I was six. My room was my friend, my constant companion and I talked to it. When our parents "broke" the news that we were moving because they bought a house, I became hysterical; I did not want to move! The last night I spent in my room I cried and apologized to my room. "This was NOT my fault!" I told it. I wanted to make sure that my room knew I had not made the choice to leave it, that the decision was forced upon me.

Back in those days, at least in our village, the kids played together by alleys. The kids living on the block on either side of the alley were your built-in playmates and met in the alley to play kick the can, red rover, sardines, freeze tag, four-square, or whatever the flavor of the day game was. Rarely were ranks broken to allow 'foreign' kids to play with us (those kids from the next block, or the next alley, or some other foreign territory).

When our family moved into our new home, I immediately became friends with the girl two doors down from me, who happened to have the same name as I. When the other kids asked me my name, I told them, "Ann." They responded, "We already have one of those; what's your middle name?"

"Teresa", I said, and thought to myself, "*I could handle that.*"

"Nope," they rejected it. "Too long; we will call you 'Teri.'"

Ugh! I *hated* that name. But, if I wanted to play, that is what I was to be called. So, 'Teri' it was!

From second grade through eighth grade, I was 'Teri' in the 'hood, but myself during school (this is my perspective on the subject). The friend I made initially on our block, Ann, was two years older than I was. At that juncture in life, there is a huge difference between a second grader and a fourth grader, and we quickly distanced from each other, but I ended up being friends with her little sister, Janice, who was one year my junior. She would eventually become my some-time best friend, some-time arch enemy and nemesis.

When I graduated eighth grade and looked forward to high school, one of the things I was *most* looking forward to was getting rid of the 'Teri' moniker. Much to my surprise (and chagrin), I sat down in my freshman Biology class, and my teacher began reading the roster for attendance; and instead of calling out "Ann", he called out "Teri".

I startled; what had not occurred to me was that the house two doors down, the house with the "original" Ann and her little sister Janice, was the house of another teacher, in the science department: Chemistry. He knew my new biology teacher very well, and although I had never met him, my biology teacher had already known me for years as 'Teri', being a teacher's kid myself and a friend of Ann's; he probably even thought I liked it.

'Teri' followed me around in high school; sporadically, but it was there enough to bug me. Then I graduated; I was heading off to college, and freedom from 'Teri', at last!

For two years I was 'Teri'-free. Then I decided that college was not for me and joined the ranks of the working world and kept my 'Teri'-free policy in place. Except this place often paged people in the warehouse for phone calls, and it was only then I realized how much "Leon", "Don", and "John" all sounded like "Ann" to me over a PA system, and I reconsidered my policy.

After changing jobs, I became a switch-hitter, name-wise. I went back to Teri and discovered I did not hate it as much as I thought. In a way, it was oddly comforting, like donning an old disfavored, but not yet discarded sweater. I could not believe I felt that way, but I did.

When I switched jobs again, I told them my real name was Ann, but that I preferred to be called Teri; imagine my surprise on the first day as I began my new position and met *the two other Terrys already working there.*

Oh, and no 'Ann's! *Sigh*

The Neighbor

In the 18th year if my life, I finally had my own apartment! It was just a studio apartment with a separate kitchen, but it was mine! And the boiler closet had enough room to house my bike; I was all set! The landlord accepted animals, so I could keep my two dogs (an Alaskan Malamute and an Irish Setter). It was a perfect set-up for me!

For my second year at U of I, I would live in my own apartment; much better than a dorm! I could keep my own schedule, 'do my own thing' (as we said back then), and nobody could tell me any differently.

And then, 'she' started acting up: the neighbor who lived immediately over my apartment. The one who insisted that 6:00 AM on Saturday morning was the appropriate time to vacuum her hardwood floors. Yes: she <u>vacuumed</u> her hardwood floors, at 6:00 AM, right over my head every Saturday morning, for a duration of a half hour. The room was only about 12 x 15: I have no clue as to why it took her so long. Maybe at that time of the day, it just seemed like a half hour; I really was not watching the clock.

Another woman moved in across from the grouch with the vacuum, and she always came in late at night, singing loudly; but she was a different kind of loud, she was happy! I expected that the two would be at loggerheads eventually, but I figured I could pop some popcorn and watch what ensued. I found out later, as the nice neighbor, Terri, and I became friends, that she was a music major and was in a musical. She practiced her role on her way home, thus the singing.

As the grouch upstairs complained to me that I was too noisy, she apparently never said a word to Terri, the singing neighbor, about her disruptive arrivals; I knew this because I asked Terri about it. However, because this was during mid-terms, I complied with the grouch's (in my opinion) unreasonable request for absolute silence.

One Saturday evening I decided to listen to my stereo. This was not something I did much anymore, as I had run into some issues with it at the dorm, also, and it just was not worth the fight. But I chose mellow that night, Dave Mason to be specific, and put on an album.

About four songs into the album, I heard a knock at my door. As my dogs traditionally both slept in front of the door, they got up and began to bark; I opened the door to a couple of uniformed officers.

Confused, I shooed the dogs away, and asked if I could help them. They exchanged an uncomfortable glance, then looked in the apartment; they saw I was alone, and I am sure both noted that we could easily converse above the noise level of the music. The one closest to me said, "Ma'am, we've had a complaint that your music is too loud, and we're here to request you turn it down." Again, he looked over at the 'offending' stereo, and seemed perplexed.

"Really? Do you feel it's too loud? Because I haven't touched the volume since I put it on."

"We have no opinion, ma'am, we're just here to relay a message."

"Let me guess: the woman upstairs called you, right?"

"Ma'am, we are not at liberty to say."

"Oh, don't worry, you don't have to: I already know."

They left, and I marched myself loudly up to her door, and firmly knocked on it. She tried ignoring it, but I was in a fit of righteous indignation, and I was not going to give up without speaking to her. I banged on the door, which she finally opened, a tiny crack, to ask what

I wanted. I told her that if she had issues with me, I would appreciate her talking to me in person and not involving the police.

She told me that she <u>tried</u> knocking on the door, but that my music was 'so loud' that I was not able to hear the knock. She told me that she was in the middle of studying for her finals and needed peace and quiet.

"*At 7:15 on a Saturday night? Dave Mason?*" I thought.

I told her that had to be a lie, because the dogs sleep in front of the door, and they certainly would have heard the knock and barked, even if I "could not". Then I took the opportunity to remind her that she had lived in the building longer than I had, and that I felt sorry for her if she was not aware of the doorbells on our mailboxes; if there was truly no response to her knock, she could have used the doorbell.

I stomped downstairs and was still fuming! I had to *do* something. So, I decided to make banana bread. (What else does one do when one is upset, right?) Of course, I was going to be in the kitchen now, so I had to turn the volume up on my stereo. Too bad, so sad, oh well.

I got my baking supplies out and started the process. Then I realized I purchased the wrong kind of nuts; I needed them chopped but had purchased halves. Darn! Hmmm. I thought of a quick on-the-spot corrective measure for this: I got out my hammer, put the bag of nuts against the kitchen wall, and began 'chopping' the nuts. Into really, really, small pieces. Probably smaller than necessary, but I felt it was appropriate, as well as therapeutic.

And after making the bread and placing it in the oven, I returned to the living room and 'forgot' to turn the volume down. Again, oops!

She moved away a couple of weeks later. I cannot believe she never even said goodbye!

The News

There was so much pain in watching my father's slow demise. Little by little I watched as his body failed him. Actions that had been second nature to him during his early life became feats of miracles as he declined. Congenital heart failure, high blood pressure, myasthenia gravis, atypical Parkinson's, metastasized prostate cancer, and hey, why not throw in a feeding tube for the fun of it, too!

These all took their toll, each in its own way, and owned my father's body. It was like watching my father's systems and body conspire, and kill him bit by bit, day by day. Watching him struggle as he tried to walk, grasp an object, talk, and even breathe; these became daily chores rather than just bodily functions performed without thought or effort in normal daily life.

Then my father's doctor, the oncologist, called for a family meeting to 'discuss various treatment options'. He had ordered a bone scan, and he wanted the family with my dad when he read the results. That was what we were told. Let me share this with you: when you get this news from your father's oncologist, your mind wanders into the darkest recesses imaginable; it is not a fun place to be!

I called the doctor's office to find out why a bone scan had been ordered; had something happened, or did he have symptoms that indicated a change in status? I was told that with prostate cancer, a bone scan is routinely done every one to two years, and that it is routine to have the family in when the results are presented to ensure that everyone is on the same page, and that if options are discussed, everyone knows what they are. Basically, to facilitate the doctor so that he does not have to go through it more than once with the family.

Whew! What a relief! I suppose somebody could have informed us, but nice to know.

My parents had been typical 50s parents and told us little about their health or their financial concerns as we grew up. So, this made sense, too; my mother had been gone almost two years now, and probably for the last scan results, it was my parents alone who were in attendance. I do recall, shortly before her death, that she told me that his cancer was back, but that was as much as I was told, probably true with my brother, Mark, as well.

I took this as good news; if this was routinely done every one to two years, and it had been two, then there was probably no real concern. This was the state of mind I had when we met with the doctor, due largely to his office personnel.

When I visited my dad, I liked to get him out and about, even if just for mundane errands. His favorite outing was a visit to the local drug store; to a man with all his ailments and issues, it was like watching a kid in a toy store. It was quite amusing, and it amazed me how quickly he could 'ditch' me when he so desired. More than once I was left wandering the aisles looking for my father; you know, the one with the walker!

But the last time I had visited, I had some issues getting my father in and out of my car, and he seemed to be transitioning into being more dependent on his wheelchair than on his walker. While I could pick up his walker, I could not lift the wheelchair to get it in and out of my car.

I discussed transportation options with my dad's nursing home for the doctor's visit. They had a van that could transport residents to and from doctor's appointments, for a fee, of course. I asked their opinion on whether they thought we could handle him and his walker. Taking his condition into account, they did not think that the walker was a good idea anymore, and they actively discouraged me from doing that.

Mark and I met my father at the home and followed the van to his appointment. That day, my father was his only office appointment, as he had surgery scheduled prior to it. The doctor was over an hour late.

I had a bout of flu the previous month and had been warned that it was one of those that came and went, and then came back when you least expected it. That morning, it was on its second RE-visit to my body, and I felt horrible. My head was stuffy, I had a headache, probably a fever too, as I was uncomfortably warm; in short, I was miserable, but this was not about me. I tried not to show my discomfort, but I am not sure I was all that successful at it. I just wanted to go home and get some sleep! But that was at least three hours away, and after the doctor finally showed up for the appointment.

He appeared at 12:20 for our 11:00 appointment, and the visit was on. We were told rather unceremoniously that my father's cancer had metastasized into his bones, but that his testosterone level was low and then something about the cancer producing testosterone, and then something about chemical castration and then...*what?*

First let me state: I am a girl. I do not care what all these newfangled women say about their bodies, I am comfortable in mine; there maybe a little too much of it, but I digress. And although I have been married, I have spent most of my adult life sans partner; as a result, I know nothing about prostates. Sorry guys, I do not have one and I was just never interested enough to research. I do not know much about the appendix either, even though I do have one.

What the prostate does, how the prostate works, and how cancer affects the prostate and the rest of the body: this was all mystery to me to begin with. Treating prostate cancer: totally clueless. And it would not bother me to remain so.

And this man is talking to us as though we are (1) familiar with my dad's situation and current treatment (again, hello? 1950s mentality? You do not discuss these things!), and (2) that after having received this kind of, I assumed, devastating news, we were supposed to sit there and discuss things civilly, as though this is just another Monday afternoon.

Between the flu, the news, and the med-speak, my head was awash in confusion. The appointment ended, and we were all in our respective worlds. The transport van was awaiting my father, and Mark and I had to get back to Chicago; but now we would be arriving in the middle of rush hour, not optimal. We quickly said our goodbyes and parted ways at this point; I guess you could say we all retreated to our own corners.

During the next couple of days, parts of the conversation came back to me. And I realized that there were two options the doctor seemed to be presenting: both relatively new, and both quite expensive. One was over $80K annually, which would put my father out on the streets! But he also spoke to us about compassionate dollars coming in, and that this is the time of year there are a lot of funds available. I do remember him saying that and leaving this meeting believing that his office was going to pursue that angle.

Frankly, when you looked at my father's overall condition, as this drug was not a 'cure' per se, I felt it was probably unconscionable to take that route with him. Even if we eliminated the cancer from the picture, my dad's condition would not perceptively improve. He would still not be able to breathe easily, to speak, to walk, to stand, to communicate, to do all those simple little things that most take for granted. His body would still be deteriorating, day by day, and the little that he could still do would slowly ebb away, regardless of this ridiculously expensive treatment. It was a sad realization that for my dad at this point, cancer would be the least critical condition to cure, or even treat.

I called my dad's nursing home and spoke with my contact there. My dad had used this facility a few years ago for a three-month rehabilitation stay, and there was one administrator that both my mother and I trusted, Kevin. I spoke with him and told him what the doctor had told us.

To say he was surprised would have been an understatement; he could not believe that anyone would suggest to my dad that a new drug therapy would be beneficial to him unless it would mitigate the pain in his bones. But Kevin said he was amazed my dad did not display signs of any pain. And the cost behind the therapy floored him as much as it had us.

He mentioned Hospice care. The last place my dad lived, a supportive living facility, left the residents as much to themselves as they could handle, with limited medical interaction. They issued pills and meds and such, but they were not allowed to help the residents take them. Even my dad with his G-Tube feedings did not receive help; he did it all. However, as he had slowly become more dependent on that facility for his care, he had basically placed himself out of that residence and into a full-fledged nursing home.

But even that former facility, the one that stressed independence, had mentioned hospice care to me. As I was moving my dad out, one of the CPNs asked if we had ever considered hospice for him. I was rather taken aback, and I said, "Oh, I don't think he's ready to go yet. I don't believe he's ready for hospice!"

She explained how hospice had changed, and that they had quite a few patients with them who had been in hospice for 3 – 4 years, and that some had even improved to the point of placing out of it. However, as I was busy, literally, moving my dad that day, I did not have time for an in-depth conversation about it. It just sat in the back of my head, until Kevin mentioned it again.

He told me all about hospice and explained how the philosophies had changed, how they are trying to intercede earlier and that it is not the end-of-life care of the days of yore. He said they worked with four different hospices, and he would be happy to provide a phone number if I wanted.

Not knowing what else to do, I took the number and called them. I was amazed! I could not believe the services available, if my dad qualified, or how much they could and would do for him. If nothing else, it was someone else to visit him two to three times a week and to check on him; something I did not have the flexibility of doing as I lived three hours away, and somebody who understood his medical needs better to keep a closer eye on him. He would have help with personal hygiene, he would have an advocate in "the system", and we could be better apprised of his day-to-day medical condition. They even find out their patients' hobbies and have volunteers come in and help them.

She told me, after speaking with me and learning of all his afflictions, even without the cancer, he would qualify for their services, although they would have to send someone out to formally assess him.

I could not believe nobody had mentioned anything about this before, and I was really wishing that we would have known about this a few years ago, when my mother was his sole caregiver and needed a reprieve. That might have also aided the quality of her life; but I digress.

I called the doctor's office for clarification. At least now I had the benefit of thinking about it for a couple of days, and I had some actual questions. Plus, I knew there was a viable option to spending all my dad's money, and then some, on a drug that did not even promise a cure, although I know that was my father's hope.

The doctor's reaction to my questions was surprising. I told him that I did not see how spending that kind of money on a non-curative drug therapy would be beneficial, and that I was a little confused between the two drug therapies he had advocated.

He was surprised that I thought he was advocating for my dad to go into these drug therapy options; that he assumed my brother and I were "sophisticated enough" to understand what he was advocating; that even to get my dad into the proper condition for entering either one of the programs would take some time and an alternate drug therapy. His suggestion was to keep things status quo.

What? I was confused.

The day of the family conference, he had begun the conversation explaining his 'watchful waiting' theory; but it seemed to me that his whole point was that time had passed beyond 'watchful waiting' and that the cancer had progressed enough to change his course of therapy. So, after I found out that I was just not "sophisticated enough" to understand his implication, I told him that I had called hospice on my father's behalf. He said good; that is what he would have done.

"Really? Because in all your 'watchful waiting' talk, I never once heard hospice as an option!" I thought to myself. I really was beginning to dislike this guy.

After he threw out a couple more insults berating our collective lack of intellectual capacity, I determined that not only was I done with him, but I did not think I should ever speak with him again. Habitually and historically, I have difficulty controlling my tongue at times I probably should, especially when I feel justified in my indignation.

After finishing my conversation with the doctor, I called Mark and said, "I want to ask you one question, and I want your first, gut reaction as an answer: When we went to the doctor's office with dad, what was the doctor advocating?"

He hesitated long enough to make me think he may not agree with my assessment (thus proving the doctor's calculation of my mental acuity accurate), but then he said, "I don't know; some nice, shiny brand, new drug therapy is what I thought."

"Thank you!" I said.

Then I told him how obviously unsophisticated we both were, brought up that if he and I left feeling that way, the chances were that was what dad thought, too. I asked Mark to free up the next Saturday he could so that we could be together to talk with dad to make sure we were all in agreement with his next step of treatment. Minimally, I wanted to make sure that he understood that, regardless of what the doctor said, he did not believe that these drug programs were appropriate for him. Long-term, I wanted to feel him out about entering a hospice program.

It was a long day. I had offered to drive and pick Mark up to minimize our efforts as well as to give us time to talk about how dad took the news, what he thought the next step should be, if my dad did not want to go into hospice, etc.

Two days before we left, I had a realization; there was a three-hour drive in which we would be together, in the same car, *prior to* seeing our dad. Why this had not occurred to me before was beyond me. I will admit that there have been times in my life I have been so focused on the goal that I do not think about some of the steps leading toward that goal until they are imminent; this was one of those times!

Although I have never understood the gulf that separated us and wondered if this was something we would ever bridge, being contained for this long together alone was something that we had not tried. I know I always wanted my big brother in my life and have never understood why he seemed to disdain me so much. Even entering our adult years, I have never understood the impetus. It was something that has always been, and I did not know how to change that. Even my mother's death had seemingly not made a dent, although I felt I had reached out to him more, I never felt it reciprocated.

But again, I had long ago resigned myself to the fact that Mark and I had one, big non-relationship. Facts were just facts. Now we have this wonderful three-hour stretch of time in which we must make small talk, or journey in silence. Small talk was something in which he does not excel, although I am usually adept at it. Until I receive mono-syl-labic answers, to virtually everything: for three hours. It got old, and finally I ceased trying.

When we arrived at the nursing home, I had arranged for us to meet with my dad in a private conference area, and for one of the hos-pice nurses to be present to explain all that hospice has become. By now, I had reconciled myself to the new face of hospice; even Mark told me that after speaking with them he asked them, "What's the downside? I'm still waiting." So far, neither of us had found one. But we had also the advantage of about eight days of acclimating to the thought of hos-pice. We still had to see where my dad stood on the issue.

We got there at the same time as the nurse, and I brought my dad into the conference room. I began by explaining to him that I had called the doctor and that, although I knew it was his fervent wish for a miracle drug and the doctor seemed as though he had been advo-cating for these new drug therapies, the doctor wanted to keep things status quo; this meant no miracle drug, and no miracle cure. I told him that both his former residence and this one had suggested to me to contact hospice, and how much hospice had changed; how much improvement they could make in his day-to-day living.

I saw my father deflate as soon as I told him what the doctor said, and when I said the word, "hospice" I saw his eyes brim with tears. He stared directly at me as one, lone tear trickled down his cheek, and broke my heart. All hope he had in this new miracle cure had vanished with that one word: hospice. And I was the one to say it.

I just prayed we were "sophisticated enough" to have made the right choice for him.

In loving memory

The Odd Maintenance
of my Carpeting

J had moved; I had not really planned on it, and I was not happy about it, but it had happened.

By way of background, my second marriage began on the rocky side. Who am I kidding? The beginning, the middle and the end were all rocky. I had met a man, Gary, on the rebound from the breakup of my first marriage; but he had two things I had always, passionately, wanted: Great Danes and macaws. This blinded me and clouded my judgment.

A few things had happened. We married, and I remember leaving the courthouse thinking, "*Should I turn around and annul this now, or ride it out.*" I think because I had just divorced my first husband, and was already disappointed with my judgment of late, I decided to ride out the course already laid. I did not make that decision "for us"; rather, I knew that I needed to ground myself again, and another major decision would not facilitate that. I had also grown attached to his animals and I would lose them if I left now; I loved them all, and they mitigated much of the pain and loneliness.

Thinking back, even on our first date, by the end I was thinking to myself, "*Just get me away from here!*". I looked back retrospectively and thought, "*I really should have trusted my gut there.*" By the time dispassionate judgment emerged we were married, and I was attempting to make the most of it, or at least, ride it out until a conclusion was foregone. Right now, even I recognized that our lives were not settled, and we had not yet played out our roles in each other's lives.

He decided to accept a buyout from the railroad; essentially, to retire. I was only 30, and he was ten years' my senior. But he was also, frankly, lazy. Quite often in the days to come it crossed my mind that he never really loved me, he needed someone to take care of the animals, which I was happy to do; I am sure he considered the money I had from selling the house after my divorce a bonus.

So, he had his buyout money, and decided we "needed" to move to southeast Missouri. Not because we had a love for the state, or even the terrain down there, but because it had cheap acreage; he was looking for a place to raise dogs and tropical birds, and figured he wanted a lot of land. If it was cheap enough, "we" could pay cash.

Initially, I joined him on a few forays searching different locations in the state; ultimately, someone was needed to take care of the animals: by now we had four Great Danes, eight Macaws, more than 14 other tropical birds, three cats, and my malamute. I volunteered to stay home. It gave me peace; I loved being alone with the animals.

My husband was a handful, and the life I was living took a toll on me. I was sure that he was emotionally abusive, but there was a niggling self-doubt in my mind that I was imagining things. I remember more than once looking into a mirror and wishing that he were physically abusive, so that I could see the abuse rather than just feel it; it was a difficult life with him there.

This was my frame of reference, and my general state of mind at the time. The animals were my refuge, and I loved them. Further, if what I suspected was true, I could not – no, make that *would not* – leave them alone with him, either; so, I felt trapped.

Meanwhile, he went to and fro searching for the "perfect" property. We sat down at the beginning of this process when it became apparent both of us could not search to prioritize our needs and wants; we knew we could not afford everything we wanted, but there were some "non-negotiables" on the list.

Such as fencing; we were preparing for our move and were adding livestock, so we now had seven Great Danes and needed a place to allow them to run. Ideally, we would have a barn, or at least an outbuilding, in which we could house the birds. Even if it was a temporary placement until we built our barn/aviary, the birds needed protection from the elements.

And then there was water, and access to electricity. Being from "The City", I would consider these standard; rural Missouri, however, was not on the same page as I. So, these two items made the list.

There were other items: acreage, preferably cleared; cross fencing; multiple outbuildings, etc.; but the non-negotiable priority was a place for us to live with water and electricity, acreage with fencing and at least one outbuilding.

He was gone for a couple of days, and it was peaceful and serene. I received a call one night: he had found the "perfect" place. Before I could respond, he clarified, "Well, you'll hate it, but it's perfect!"

I had once been told that I had a way of beginning a conversation that ended it; apparently, Gary was vying for the prize! Great conversation starter, Gary!

OK, so let us start with: does it have fencing? *No.*

Then I guess there is no cross fencing? *No.*

Is there an outbuilding? *No; we would have to build it.*

Is there water or electricity? *There is a 325 ft. well, and no electricity access for a building.*

OK, so how is the house? Does it have at least two bedrooms? *No. It is a 16-year-old trailer, but it has two bedrooms and a tip-out.*

Why don't we move to the positives: what makes it perfect? *The price. We can afford it.*

"OMG – REALLY?" I thought.

Then he told me that he was going to come home Friday night to pick me up so that we could travel eight hours through the night to see it and I could decide for myself whether it was 'perfect'. During this conversation, he got excited about the place, and he slipped, mentioning the closing at 9:00 AM on Saturday.

Closing?

"So, that means you've already made your decision; you have made an offer; which they have accepted. You have even already involved the bank, and a title company; what difference does it make whether I see it or not; you are buying it!"

He realized his error and tried to sweet talk me into not being mad; but I believe he confused feeling irrelevant with being mad. I had just realized that my husband did not care to seek my opinion before making such a large decision and purchase; I was hurt. Again.

I told him there was no need for him to come back; I did not have to see it. It did not matter. He had made his decision, and the eight-hour drive each way was, in my opinion, redundant. He told me he was coming to get me, regardless, as my opinion was now suddenly of paramount importance to him.

This was Tuesday, and I was not looking forward to Friday, as I had this sneaking suspicion that he was going to show up highly charged; I was dreading it.

Friday night, well after dark, I saw headlights in the driveway; I had a physical reaction to seeing him, and it was not a pleasant one. I knew he was furious at me for some imaginary infraction or another, and for the first time in our relationship I was afraid of what he may do.

He came in like a tornado: all whirling and emotional. He was as a force of nature, and when he was mad there was no reasoning with or talking to him; he just had to ride it out on his own. He was screaming and got in my face, at which point, I turned and walked into the bedroom. He followed me, yelling and screaming every vitriol he could think to hurl.

I got out a box and began packing while he was screaming at me. I realized how sad it was that I had brought so little with me to live here, and I thought that maybe there had been a subconscious reason for that. It suddenly occurred to him what I was doing, which calmed him down a bit.

Eventually, we were able to talk, and he even talked me into going down to the property with him to see it. He promised me that if I did not like it, we would not have to close; he had arranged for me to see it at 7:30 AM, prior to the closing.

Somewhere during this discussion, I called my parents to ask that they meet us in Missouri. I wanted their opinion on the place, as I now realized I was in no shape to make a rational decision; he was right, I was going to hate the place, but what he did not realize was that this was his own self-fulfilling prophecy. He had already made me hate it, sight unseen.

They agreed to meet us down there; we arranged a meeting place, and we were off on our eight-hour junket to our 'new home'. Yay.

Between the circumstances and the hour, there really was not much chit chat, and I honestly cannot say that I was happy to be there, with my husband; I felt like anything but a wife. We pulled into town near 7:00 AM, he gave me a quick tour of the town, then it was off to see the trailer at 7:30; I cannot say it was enchanting, but it was not quite the hell that I had pictured. It was just that I felt I had no say, and no choice; that was my biggest resistance.

The property itself was secluded: set in a gully, fronting a national or state park, so there was a lot of timber behind us. The trees were young, for the most part saplings, with a few mature trees. There was an elevated pond, which I assumed was man-made. Walking around the trailer, I figured out what a "tip-out" was: it was an extension to the trailer that added an extra four or five feet to the living area, and that was where the wood stove had been placed.

Not that we could use it, because of the birds. They do not have lungs, they have air sacs, and we needed to watch our heating options, as well as any cleaning products we used. Until we could clear a quarter acre or so to build a barn, we would be living with the birds, in the trailer. And the dogs.

Thankfully, the cats were outdoor cats. We had twenty-six tropical birds, their cages and seven Danes. The malamute had a hard time integrating into the Dane community, as she always instigated fights; but there was an old, small outbuilding not much larger than an out-house that could afford her shelter behind the trailer, until we could better accommodate her.

We knocked on the trailer, as it was now 7:30. As I expected, there was no answer. So now, yes, officially, we would be buying a property, literally, sight unseen on my part. The trailer was old, as I said, but did look like it had been well-maintained. I would still have preferred to see the inside as well.

We left for the closing; I had talked myself into giving this a try, as horrible as the circumstances were and with my gut feeling of doom, and we signed the papers. Immediately after that, we needed to leave to meet my parents; but we made plans, again, to see the trailer upon our return.

We met my parents, who then followed us and ultimately were going to drive me back home, as I had animals to attend. Gary was going to stay to begin the process of clearing an area and lining up material deliveries to begin construction.

We got to the trailer, and this time (now that we owned it) there was a response to our knocks. They let us in, and it was so dark and depressing that I began to choke back tears. I looked around to see if there was any positive thing I could say, but there was not.

Having been manufactured in the mid-70s, the trailer was decorated with dark wood paneling and brown shag (yes – *SHAG*) carpeting; there was no sunlight, nothing bright in the house to break up the browns in the décor. And the canopy of trees overhanging the trailer filtered out any sunlight, leaving an atmosphere of gloom.

I am sure I walked through the place like a zombie; I was biting my tongue, literally, trying to contain my emotions. I took things in, but my mind screamed at me *"Get me out of here! Get me OUT!!!!".* I asked if I could use the restroom, went in and turned the water on. When there was sufficient noise, I let myself go.

I felt as if my soul was screaming, even as I was trying to minimize any noise I made. I cried harder than I remembered crying in a long, LONG time. I know my mother had noticed I was gone, but I could still hear my husband chit-chatting with the, now, tenants of the property. I had to pull myself together. The last thing I wanted to do was to insult these nice people: none of this was their fault!

I cleaned myself up, splashed some cold water on my face, and returned to the tour, such as it was. I mean, it was a trailer: how much was there to see?

I know my mother noticed me going into the bathroom, and I suspected she knew what I was doing. My dad and my husband were busy talking with the people, so my mother joined me outside where we could tour by ourselves and talk. She asked me how I was doing. I said, "You saw the place. How do you think I'm doing?" And she hugged me.

I composed myself and looked around. The property really was beautiful, if not sunny. Since we backed up to the state forest, it was densely timbered. And the trailer was situated at the bottom of gently rolling hills. Circumstances aside, the setting was serene.

And anyway, what was I going to do? It was ours.

Gary arranged with the former owners as to when we could start to bring our belongings and our animals down and settle in. I think they were just asking for a week to relocate, which was more than reasonable.

It was a long, and quiet, ride home. My parents, while sympathetic, knew that this was my life. They may not be any happier about it than I was, but at least they were being supportive in their silence; I was greatly appreciative of that.

I spent the next week preparing our house for sale and trying to get everything together for our move. There was a lot to consider, not the least of which was logistics in getting the animals down to their new home, eight hours away. After all, it was not only transporting the animals, but we also had to have travel-friendly containers, bring their cages and their supplies; there was a lot to consider and coordinate.

Gary could have paid cash for the property with his buy-out, but he wanted to have working capital for the construction of the barn. In essence, although we had the money, we were still financing the whole move and purchase while neither of us was working while continuing to financially maintain our empty Chicago house until its sale. And it was not even yet on the market.

"*Take a deep breath; one issue at a time.*" I reminded myself.

Eventually, and with gargantuan effort on the parts of my parents, our attorney, our realtor and me, everything was done, settled, and we were ready to make the final move. My husband had gone down a few days earlier with a few dogs and all the birds. He was setting them up while I prepared the house prior to sale. That done, my three favorite dogs and I we were off to our new home.

I had taken the eight-hour trip quite a few times, but the dogs were not used to riding that long, so we roamed around and took a lot of breaks. I was so "excited" about getting to our new home that I flirted with the idea of taking the dogs to a park in East St. Louis;

even I knew that was an invitation to trouble, but the thought really did cross my mind!

We meandered and made our way to our new home, and I let them loose into their new pen. Although we had a rather large yard by Chicago standards, it was nothing compared to what we had now. The "pen" we were using for the dogs was about a quarter to a half-acre, all by itself. They almost did not know what to do with all that space!

Then I went into the house, er, trailer. We had birds on the front porch, birds in each room and one of the two bedrooms that we did have was totally dedicated to them. Cage on top of cage, floor to ceiling, and wall to wall. I do not know if any of you have ever owned birds, but they are not the most hygienic of creatures to have. Quite the opposite, I should say. They like to play in their water; they like to throw their food and seed around; they have fun making a mess! They seem to delight in it even more if they sense that it bothers you, too. Nobody can tell me that they do not understand what they are doing or saying!

All animals inside, combined with the depressing interior of the trailer, was difficult for me to handle. And, although I cleaned the cages daily, I tried not to be around the birds in the dedicated bird room. We had some birds from the Amazon family, and they are known for producing a soft talc-like powder which protects their feathers; unfortunately, the powder does not stay on their feathers. It permeates everything, and ends up everywhere.

After living in this situation for about a month, and seemingly being on this merry-go-round of cleaning and picking up after animals that have no sense of appreciation for a clean environment, I noticed something strange. Something that I had never seen before...my carpeting was growing weeds!

Really? This is my life? It has devolved into **weeding my shag carpet.**

Could I at least have a current style of carpeting to weed? Like, a Berber, maybe?

The Park

Growing up, we lived across the street from a locally popular play park in our town. My dad decided to take me and my brother, Mark, there one Sunday to play. I was three and my brother was five, so we each held one of my dad's hands to cross the busy street.

After crossing, Mark, being the elder, immediately dropped my dad's hand and took off running to the merry-go-round. Back then, they were all made of wood and metal. He jumped onto it and, like any self-respecting child of the times, rode with his legs hanging on the outside, ready to mobilize at a moment's notice. I, on the other hand, having been placed on the merry-go-round by my protective father, had my legs hanging properly into the middle, as they should, so that I could hold on to the handle as the merry-go-round turned. As soon as I was settled on the ride, my brother jumped off and ran to the swing set.

Being the ever-adoring little sister, I wanted to follow my big brother to the ride he was on, so I jumped off to run to the swing set, too; except I was on the business side of the wood and metal merry-go-round. I realized as it conked me on the head that I had made a mistake, and I had the expected three-year-old response to pain: I cried. My dad picked me up, held and comforted me until I calmed down, and then he took me to the swing set and sat me in the swing next to my big brother.

He took turns pushing us; first me, then my brother, then back to me. But Mark wanted to go on to bigger and better things, so he jumped off the swing to run to the slide. Not wanting to be left out, I did too. But I was unfamiliar with the concept of jumping from the swing on the uptick; I just let go, and it did not work out quite as well for me as it did my brother. I landed on my back, knocking out my breath, and with another conk on the noodle. And my dad, once again, held and comforted me. And probably began to wonder exactly why he ventured out with us that day, too, but he never said anything.

Once I was calm again, we decided to join my brother on the slide. It was an old metal slide, with dual metal guardrails at the top. I distinctly remember my dad saying, "There is *NO WAY* I am letting anything happen to you on this. Let me go up first, and then you can sit in my lap, and we'll go down together." I was, of course, thrilled at this prospect, so I anxiously awaited him situating himself and then telling me I could climb up. He reached behind, lifted me up and set me directly on his lap.

I was absolutely in Daddy Princess heaven!

We started down the slide, and I do not remember exactly how it all happened; but the next thing I knew was that he sailed out from underneath me, and I was left hanging upside down by my left knee. Neither one of us realized, as I was sitting on my dad's lap, that my left leg was hanging off the side of the slide; the slide with those guardrails I mentioned, the ones that went halfway down the slide.

I can tell you from experience that they will hold an upside down, screaming three-year-old until her dad rescues her, yet again!

It was at that point that my dad decided that maybe we should cut our visit short; "before he killed me", I believe is how he put it. I remember him waiting an exceptionally long time to cross the street; I think he waited until he did not see anything moving at all in either direction before he crossed the busy street with us.

Funny, I do not remember going to the park with him, ever again!

The Pediatrician

J have had a lifelong struggle with my weight, but beginning in about 6th grade, I really began to balloon out. I would hear people say to my parents, "She's big, but at least she's proportionate." Or "She's so big-boned!" Or my favorite, "At least she has a pretty face!"

Were these supposed to be consolation prizes? That I may be fat, but not to worry, I am fat all over? Even at ten, I knew that "big boned" was adult-speak for "fat". And apparently fat people are not supposed to be pretty, so I guess I was lucky?

Then my mother began trying to help me by nagging whenever she saw me eating something I liked (in other words, junk food). My knee jerk (and, in my mind, totally reasonable) reaction was to open the fridge, and basically eat everything in it that did not walk away from me.

By 8th grade, I was 5'4" tall, and weighed in at a whopping 197 pounds; and that was after fasting for two full days because I knew I had an upcoming physical scheduled for high school.

Oops!

I waded through my freshman year of high school in a self-imposed fog, not wanting to stand out (in my experience, standing out was never a good thing) and trying to maintain a low profile. But at the end of my freshman year, something began happening to me.

I realized that my clothes were just a tad looser on me, and that it was not so much of a chore to move around. And I discovered jazzercise! I loved it, Disco aside.

During my sophomore year, I asked if I could take some extra exercise or dance classes during my study halls; no credits attached, just audit the courses. Effectively, I was taking a minimum of two gym classes per day. My day began with an hour of exercise at home, followed up by two or three hours more after school, prior to starting my homework; then as many exercise classes as I could fit in during the day.

I really started to see a drop in weight, and one day in the shower I realized that I had found my hip bones, for the very first time! This also had a strange side benefit to me, as boys began to notice me. Not run from me or make fun of me, as before, but to pay attention to me, and wanting to be around me. I was not used to that! With my experience, I was wary of that.

I recall my dad telling me in jest one time, "I really liked so-and-so in high school, until I found out that she liked me; then I wondered what was wrong with her." I knew he was joking, unfortunately, that was exactly how I felt; except I was not kidding.

One day near the end of sophomore year, I was walking down the hall in one of my pretty new, little dresses toward my friend, Nancy. She stood there, with an odd look on her face, and I watched her cock her head as she looked at me. When I was close enough to her, I asked her what was she was doing, and she asked, "Where'd the rest of you go? You have lost about half of you, and I just realized it."

I went home that day and stepped on the scale. One thirty-five! And I was no longer 5'4", I was 5'9". Now that I felt there was a light at the end of the tunnel, I was on a mission; I was determined to lose more weight!

At the height of my anorexia, I did not know what it was, but I recognized the symptoms after I saw three of my friends near the end of our junior year walking through the hall. Three friends from three different groups of kids; all of them looked to me like nothing more than walking skulls. I asked around to find out what was wrong with them and received the same answer each time: *Anorexia*.

I did a bit of research and realized that I was probably going to have to eat a little more than my five bites of vegetables at lunch each day to keep up my health. I was pretty much living on that, exercise, caffeine and nicotine.

Our school was "open campus", meaning that Juniors and Seniors were free to come and go as they pleased on their off periods. I opted to take more dance and exercise classes when I was not on the mall smoking. I was into the whole Olivia Newton John "Physical" look: leotards, tights, leg warmers, etc. And, being a passionate student, I got to class in record time, and often had to await the rest of my class.

One day, alone in the dance studio awaiting my peers' arrival, I noticed something odd about my looks. Being a Swede, and more "large boned" than others my age, I had been working on trying to get rid of thigh rub, which, by the way, I still had at 128 pounds. In studying my body, I realized I was going to have to go home and take some measurements; something seemed 'off'.

When I got home, I measured. I had a 25-inch waist, but each thigh was 23 inches. *EACH!* In trying to get smaller, more shapely legs, I had built the muscles up to gargantuan proportion! I looked ridiculous, in my opinion, and now I knew why my reflection had seemed so 'off'!

For the first time in my life, I determined I needed to *gain* weight, just enough to become proportionate. I had learned my lesson with anorexia, and that was not a concern anymore. Eventually, I settled in at 135–140 pounds, and I was happy there. For my height, and with the amount of muscle I was carrying, this was perfect for me, and I was a size 5!

However, the battle with my weight had long-term effects on my body. I was still heavily addicted to both caffeine and nicotine, and my stomach was constantly in pain; to the point where I carried around antacids and referred to them as my 'after dinner mints'.

Concurrently, I was experiencing massive headaches. I grew up with a mom who constantly suffered from sinus issues, and it was not unusual for me to come home and find her on the couch, trying to sleep off her headache.

I devised a different approach: I wore sunglasses, almost constantly, to avoid exposure to light. When my headache became too severe, I would down my own concoction 'miracle cure': three aspirins, two Excedrin and one contact, all at once. That never failed to knock out my headache; unfortunately, I believe it also knocked out my stomach.

My mom thought I should see a doctor, but there was a doctor shortage in the 70s and you basically had to 'know somebody' to either acquire or change doctors. My mother tried to get me in to see her doctor, as I was seventeen, but that did not work, so I ended up at my pediatrician's office.

Well, not _my_ pediatrician; I saw the woman to whom he was selling his practice, and this was our first meeting.

She walked into the exam room and opened our conversation with, "You are 10 pounds' overweight."

To which I said, "No, I'm not."

"Yes, you are."

I looked at her and said a little more forcibly, "No. I am not."

"Yes, you are!"

I was studying her and thinking: _I'm seventeen—what's your excuse?_"; but I said, "No. I'm not."

"Yes, you are."

"OK, lady. I'm ten pounds' overweight; what are you going to do about it?"

"Well, just so that you know, you are ten pounds' overweight."

I said, "For your information, I was down to 128, and I looked terrible. I tried hard to gain enough weight to look normal and proportionate but remain slender; and that is at 140. I am happy here." In the back of my mind, I was thinking *"Have you ever even <u>heard</u> of anorexia?"* which seemed to be more her bailiwick than actual doctoring!

"Fine. But for the record, you're ten pounds' overweight!"

"Fine." I stared at her.

She finally asked why I was there, and I told her that I suspected I had an ulcer. She asked no questions, completed no exam, nor did she take any family history; she simply stated, "You're too young to have an ulcer."

Yay! That's it! Great! We're Done! I was so glad all my problems were solved with this one conversation; I did not have an ulcer because I was too young, and all I had to do was lose 10 pounds. That clears up everything. No more pain for me, no-siree-bob!

I stared at her for a while wondering exactly what kind of a char-latan she was. Forget the fact that I have never met this woman; forget the fact that she never took a family history and was not aware that my dad had had one ulcer, my mom had two; forget the fact that she never examined me, nor asked any questions about symptoms, lifestyle or why exactly I was there, suspecting I had an ulcer; the woman was just a fool.

As she did not have me disrobe, I was so angry with her that I just jumped off the exam table and walked past her toward the door. As I exited the room, I told her that I would be sure to tell my friend Debbie that, regardless of what <u>Debbie's</u> doctors said about her being on her **fifth** ulcer by the age of twelve, MY doctor told me Debbie is 'just too young' to have one, so she obviously does not."

I opened the door to exit, and my mother was standing outside. I turned back toward the doctor but said to my mom, "You would be a fool to pay for this appointment; it was worthless." And walked out.

My mom never asked me anything about it, and I never did see a doctor about ulcers; but then again, I did not need to: I was "too young".

The Pet

J have always been an animal person; it did not matter what brand, type or gender, if it was not human, I loved it – no qualifiers! I wanted a pet of my own of any kind so badly I decided to make up my own rules.

I was about four, and I was on a mission: I wanted a pet, and a pet I would have!

I discovered what I considered to be the perfect pet; it would need no cage, no crate, no container, or even any time out in the yard. I did not have to feed it or walk it, I just needed to love it. Why had I not thought of this before? I picked up my new pet and tried to sneak into the house with it.

My parents, ever vigilant, saw me sneaking in the back door holding my hands behind my back, scooting sideways with my back to the kitchen wall, facing them and watching them intently.

"What'chya got there, kiddo?"

"Oh, nothing..."

My dad took me by the shoulders and turned me around. "A dead bird? What in the world are you doing with a dead bird?"

"He's my perfect pet, Daddy, and I want him!" I cried.

My dad told my mom to take me into the bathroom and wash my hands to get any lice off them (I thought that was a disease). We spent the next few minutes washing my beautiful pet off my hands.

My dad came back, empty handed, and I was empty-hearted.

I scoured the neighborhood, and it did not take long before I found him in the neighbor's garbage. I was terribly upset that my dad would throw my pet away as though he was garbage, but I was happy to be able to rescue him a second time.

I walked into the kitchen again, hands behind my back, and my parents looked at me. My dad said, "You really didn't, did you? What's behind your back?" "Oh, nothing..."

So, the cycle repeated. This time, however, my mother was instructed to keep me inside until he came back, which she did. As soon as I was released, I spent the rest of the day looking for my lost pet. I never did find him. Or her?

That was OK; for in the meantime, I had devised a better plan. I would have something that could not get sick with lice, whatever that was, and was more readily available.

That night, after everybody was asleep, I tip-toed into the kitchen, and opened the fridge. Seriously, why had I not thought of this before, because it was the perfect solution (again)! I took two eggs – notice, I said two, I wanted my pets to have a companion – and I put them under my pillow. In the morning, I knew I would have two little chicks chirping away at me, and I would finally have my pets; I was just going to have to remember to keep my hands under my pillow to keep them warm!

But in the morning, I did not have two pets; I looked down at my bedroom rug and discovered all I got for my trouble was a huge mess. I had no clue as to how to clean it up, so I did the next best thing, for a four-year-old; I placed my doll's blanket very carefully over the mess covering it completely and patted it down. That was a perfect solution!

Until about a week later, when my mom tried to pick my doll's blanket up from the floor and could not. I do not think she agreed with my cleaning procedures; I suspect she felt I could have done better.

But, in the meantime, it <u>had</u> accomplished one thing: it took my mind off my obsession with pets!

Well, temporarily!

The Pitter Patter of Little Tiny Feet

I have always loved dogs, and somewhere in late grade school, I fell in love with Alaskan Malamutes, because of 'Babe'. She was a resident at our local animal shelter, if you could call it that. A malamute mix, with one floppy ear, and an obviously blind eye.

But to me, she was gorgeous!

I wanted her so badly, except as my parents pointed out, we already had a dog. She was a family dog, not "my" dog, and to me, there was a world of difference.

However, as would happen with pre-teens, my campaign diminished as my attention span waned, and I eventually gave up the fight. I was still, however, ardent about finding her a home, because the shelter she was in was a 'kill' shelter, and I could not abide that thought.

Eventually, she ended up in a storefront owned by my friend Laura's father, as a 'guard dog'. Within a week, though, Laura told me that the store had been burglarized, but the only thing missing was 'Babe'. Well, I tried! I am hoping that they wanted her badly enough to give her a great home!

I became a passionate fan of all things malamute!

While I was at college, a friend of mine told me that he was in the market for a husky. "A husky?" I asked. "Why a husky?" I was offended, because in my mind, malamutes were so much the superior breed!

I got him to agree to at least go look at a litter of malamutes, which I had conveniently already located. We got to the middle of a cornfield and found the 'breeders. A little farmhouse, with an outbuilding where they housed a male and female malamute who obliged their owners occasionally by breeding.

There were two female black and white pups, about 4-1/2 months old who were virtually identical. They both had strong masks, and those masks ran in a stripe to their noses. But one had a white "racing stripe" that ran down the center of the black stripe to her nose; that is the one I liked, because of the racing stripe.

Although they were adorable (and cheap), Tim decided against either of them. Turns out, husky fans are as strongly rooted in their feelings of fidelity as us malamute fans, and he had a husky growing up. I have a theory on that: I believe that the two breeds are so similar, that the differences become necessarily exaggerated in our minds so that the husky fan will never migrate into malamute territory, and vice-versa. I have found similar feelings in Swedes v. Norwegians; I am Swedish.

So, Tim and I were at a standoff; but I could not walk away. I bought her, the one with the racing stripe who had engaged my heart and brought her home.

It was not until we were driving home that I thought about the call I needed to make to my parents, as I was a college student and really did not have my own place for her to live, either at college or at home. I had already absorbed one stray puppy over whom they had not given me any grief. So now I would have two, neither one small, and I was not sure whether they (or I) would be welcome at their home again.

I would put that thought on the back burner for now; I was excited to have a puppy again!

And it became obvious quickly to me when we got 'home' that I also had some exceptionally large issues to handle, as she seemed not to be socialized. I was going to have my hands full with this one: training was going to be particularly difficult!

But she was sweet, and my heart went out to her in a way it had not to the stray I had picked up. The stray, my Irish Setter, McCabe, was totally self-sufficient and, although we had a strong bond, I never felt like he 'needed' me. I always felt that it was his choice to remain with me, so he did. He did love me, but he did not 'need' me.

This little baby did. She was so sweet and wanted so badly to reach out to us and please us, but she had no clue how to do so. She had never been taught to trust a human; she did not distrust humans; she was just unfamiliar with them. I had to become her teacher and her interpreter, but first I would have to break through and learn to communicate with her myself.

Temba Woulfe

We forged a much stronger bond in a much shorter time than I ever did with McCabe, and her innate strength of instinct due to the lack of socialization inspired her name: Temba Woulfe, a play on

Timber Wolf. And now that it had been a week or so, and the bonds had been forged, I needed to place a call to my parents to break the news: "*Guess who's coming to dinner?*"

Initially my call was very awkward because I was nervous and distracted. How would they take my news? Would they ban my babies from visiting? What was I going to have to do for the summer, as it was quickly approaching, and I might have to make a choice between home and them? Was I going to need to figure out what to do with them while I was home?

Finally, during that very awkward conversation, I just blurted out, "Mom, dad: I have some news."

Silence.

"I took a friend to see a litter of malamutes; he didn't get one, but I did."

Initially, silence, then a sigh of relief. "Is that all?" I remember my mother saying, as she laughed.

It was then that I understood where their minds had taken them when I told them I had news, and I realized that I probably could not have planned this approach better if I tried! They had no problems with me bringing the whole herd with me when I came home, including the cat.

Well, at least not then.

The PoPo

There have been times in my life when my 'blonde' is on full display, for all to enjoy.

Do not get me wrong: I believe anybody in the world *can be* 'a blonde', and as one, I am calling 'privilege' to be politically incorrect. There *are* honorary blondes, of which I have known many.

But I have noticed that when I am stressed, pressed for time, or have a multitude of things on my mind, my 'blonde' emerges and tends to be enhanced. I am often left laughing; generally, at my own expense, but laughing, nonetheless.

One day I had a list of errands to run, and I had to beat the closing time of the post office. In all its brilliance, my city decided to control traffic by making streets one-way. Generally, every other street is one way north or south, except for the busy streets.

For whatever reason, they made the post office almost inaccessible without having a scouted route. Best case scenario, you only need to venture four blocks out of your way, then *hope* that you can find a parking space. Worst case: you end up driving in frustrating circles and literally driving yourself crazy, as I was currently doing.

But parking is the other issue; unless you have a residential parking pass for that specific area of town, you cannot park near the post office except for the eight dedicated spaces directly in front of the building, for a population of over 56,000 people. Makes total sense to me!

Now add in construction: my favorite season. The time when all my hard-sought, tried-and-true short-cut routes are infected with closures and/or barricades, and you cannot get there from here. At all.

I was engaged in trying to figure out (1) how to get to the post office, and (2) where to park, all while dodging barricades and temporary closures, and trying hard not to think of all the other errands I needed to finish before I could go home.

I hit barricade after barricade, wrong-way after wrong-way, before I finally decided to just risk it, and make a U-turn (also illegal) to get to the stupid post office.

I got to the corner, a traffic light, with my left turn signal blinking. At the last minute and mainly because there was oncoming traffic approaching, I chickened out of making the U-turn and turned left onto the side street; this intersection is one angled street meeting a busy highway, while crossing a second angled street at the same time.

That second angled street is the one I was now driving on, and where I ultimately decided to make my illegal U-turn, rather than on the busier angled street. This secondary street is of course one way; and I realized that a little too late, and after I had completed my U-turn. And the one-way was not the way in which I was facing.

Directly across the street from me, stopped at the red light facing me, was a squad car.

Of course.

When the light turned green, I decided just to sit and wait for his approach and tried to gather my thoughts for the inevitable upcoming encounter. He pulled next to my car and rolled down his window. Taking his lead, I rolled mine down, too.

See? I am cooperating!

He just looked at me and said, "Humor me."

My mind raced and I was trying to figure out how to handle this situation, when I realized that all too much time had passed; I needed to say *something*.

But when I looked at him again, I just busted out laughing, and said, "I'm sorry. I got nothin'!"

I think that woke him up (and I am certain I caught a smirk on his face). He looked at me, and I could almost read his mind: "*Did she really just say that?*" I could tell he was also incredulous.

Rather than dealing with me, he just shook his head derisively and said, "Get outta here," effectively dismissing me.

Which I was incredibly happy to oblige, but then I was left with a conundrum: *When facing the wrong way on a one-way street at a red light, is it legal to turn right on red?*

Where's Barney when you need him?

The Practice Date

*A*fter my short jaunt at college, I came back to my hometown and even though my collegiate career had been short-circuited, I had a broader vision of life than when I left. After all, that is what college is supposed to do for you: to broaden your horizons. A least, it used to be. I came back 'ungraduated', but ready to conquer the world on my own terms.

Terms which seemed to involve Denny's a whole bunch. Inevitably, no matter where we went, no matter what we did, we ultimately ended at Denny's. It had a lot to do with the fact that most of us were smokers (at least, the ones who had cars available) and because all of us were dead broke. For the price of one cup of coffee, Denny's allowed us to socialize pretty much all night. Especially if you got to know the wait staff, which we did.

At some point in the visit, I would need a refill; I got in the habit of helping not only myself to the coffee, but I would wander around the restaurant to see if anybody else needed a top off. I have no idea if this was appreciated or unwelcome by the wait staff, but hey, I wanted a refill and got tired of waiting; I figured others might be in the same boat. Regardless, no one ever said anything to me, and my fellow customers seemed to appreciate it.

We got to know the staff well, and for the most part, embraced them in our conversations. We bantered with them, flirted with them, and generally just enjoyed being with them. They became part of our 'Denny's experience' and upon occasion, one of us would date one of the wait staff.

Which happened to me. One of the young waiters, Kieva, became enamored with me, and although not my usual type, he was handsome and a nice person, so I figured why not? Once I accepted, we referenced our schedules and decided on the day. Truthfully, I have never used a calendar in my life, and I never plan too far ahead, so finding a free night for me was not all that unusual; apparently, he was more popular than I. Or maybe just more forgetful.

The night of the date, I watched him walk up our sidewalk from upstairs. Living with my parents, my normal mode of operation was to meet whomever where we were going. Kieva would not abide that, however, and insisted that he pick me up at my house, which entailed "meeting the parents". Already. In my opinion, a little premature, but if he could endure it, I guess I could too.

By the time my parents called me downstairs, they had made their own introductions, and I noticed that he was wearing a suit jacket. Hmmm. Again, not what I was used to, and frankly, a tad off-putting to me, but whatever.

We got in the car, and he took me downtown to an upscale diner for dinner. A place that I had never heard about before, but a winner in my book! I mentioned that at dinner and received a rather odd reply: that was the same reaction that his 'practice-date' had to the place.

Practice-date?

"What is that?" I asked him. He explained that, before he brought me to this restaurant, he and a friend (male) had come to try the restaurant out to see if it was good enough for me.

Uh, huh.

In my humble opinion, part of the overall experience of dating was to take your date to places that you love and/or that mean something to you. Contrarily, if you decided to try something new, try it out together, and have the experience, good or bad, be a shared one. But to go on a 'practice date' with a same-sex friend? OK, now we have ventured into kind of creepy territory.

I thought about everything combined: the insistence of picking me up at my home; showing up in a dinner jacket; meeting the parents on the first date; not only taking someone on a practice date, but then actually admitting it to me. I was uncomfortable, and I wanted to go home, although I had not yet conveyed anything negative.

Kieva had no idea what was going through my head, so after we finished dinner and left the restaurant, he drove around downtown for a bit. He ended up parking at a spot by the lake. Now, he could have said, "To see the beautiful skyline;" he could have said, "Just to have a few minutes to talk." But no, he went right for it: he wanted to "watch the submarine races".

Alright, it is official; I am no longer amused and totally creeped out. I needed to get home.

I cannot remember exactly how I extracted myself, but I do know there were no submarine races. And there were no more dates with him. I would continue my tried-and-true practice of meeting people at our destination; at least that way I knew I would have my own way home, and in my own time.

Years later, in retrospect, I had a greater appreciation for his actions. He was just coming from a different place than I; he was socially conservative, and more considerate of familial obligations. I finally realized that most of what he did was sweet; I was just not ready for it.

I sure would not mind finding him again!

The Prophecy

After my mother passed suddenly, we all assumed that my father would quickly follow suit; after all, he had been in a slow decline for over a decade, and had recently become more and more dependent on my mother, emotionally as well as physically. So, my daughter Savanna and I, having recently sold our home, leased an apartment from our realtor and I told him that we would be the most temporary tenants he would ever have; I anticipated leaving both the apartment and the state within three to six months. I did not think there was even a remote possibility that my dad would last longer than that, and once he was gone, there was nothing holding us there anymore.

But he shocked us all and stayed with us for another three years; it was amazing to see how strong his hold on life had become. Once he did succumb, my daughter and I began our search for our new home. Although I had planned on moving to Texas with my mother, she put a damper on that by passing away. With my mom out of the picture, Savanna began a campaign to sway me away from Texas; not because of anything other than her abhorrence of hot weather.

I told her if she wanted me to move somewhere else, she would have to do the research and sell me on it. She did her research, created her little spreadsheet and sat me down; she explained the parameters she used, and gave me the pros and cons of her decision that Indiana would be "the place" for us to live.

At some point Illinois had taken, or had threatened to take, yet another of our natural rights away (I can't remember which, there have been so many), and both Mike Pence and Scott Walker took full advantage of governing border states to Illinois; they both launched anti-Illinois campaigns, but I felt Gov. Pence was more clever with his slogan, "Ill-annoyed yet?" aptly placed on the Illinois/Indiana border. So, I was not inclined to discourage her after her hard work and conclusion.

We took a weekend to travel the state and see where in the state we would want to reside. I figured if we traveled from Chicago to Evansville and back, we should get pretty much the full flavor of the state; beginning around Dana/Montezuma in Midwest Indiana, the terrain became woodsy with gently rolling hills. I could envision living in such a beautiful area, so when we got back, I began a computer-based search for real estate centering around the Wabash Valley region, which is huge.

I figured with all the "wants" we had, along with our limited resources, it would take a good two years to fulfill our wish list within our budget, so we began our search immediately. It was funny, even to me, to watch my progression; as a lifelong city dweller, I told Savanna initially that we had to have at least a half-acre of land. Once I started looking at actual properties (virtual, so far), I realized that did not even get us out of town! So, the land size increased to a full acre.

But even that seemed somehow claustrophobic, and I increased it to three-to-five acres, where it remained for the duration of our search.

In retrospect, the list of properties I put together for our realtor, Jen, to show us should have dissuaded the most dedicated realtor from working with us. In Chicago, mileage is only a sometime inconvenient factor, multiple properties 30 or so miles away from each other is no big deal, and generally quickly accessible by highway, expressway, or tollway.

I really did believe that I was keeping properties conveniently located for our search; I was, however, not familiar with country roads, and did not realize that our original listing of desired properties to see would have taken us the better part of a week, not the two days we had allotted.

Jen, ever the professional, kept her opinions to herself and tried her best to accommodate our whims. I was disappointed our first day out with her because out of the eight properties I thought we were going to see that day, we only got in to see four or five. However, her point was subtly made because of the time even that took. Reality was beginning to take hold.

And the properties we saw within our budget were just depressing! We would be spending the rest of our lives working on some of them, and still not have enough time to see them achieve livability status. I could handle some work, but my partner in "fixer uppers" (my dad) was gone; my knowledge in that regard was limited, and mostly concentrated in the areas of my interests: woodworking/carpentry and décor; that was just not going to cut it in some of these properties!

We spent two solid days with her and found absolutely nothing to even revisit. Keep in mind, I had allotted two years for this search, and we were dispirited after only two days! Savanna and I decided on the spur of the moment to search a different area of Indiana, and our realtor had to "relinquish" this search to other realtors, as it was truly out of her territory. She arranged for us to see those properties the following day with an alternate realtor and wished us luck; she would be busy hosting her son's 12th birthday party, and thus, unavailable anyway.

We checked into a hotel near our new target area. I told Savanna I was sick of house hunting and wanted to just space out to TV that night; she was exhausted and went straight to sleep. However, the hotel had an internet connection, and I had my tablet with me. Our phones had not worked all day, and I wanted to check my email.

Of course, while I was at it, I found a website I had never seen before: Land and Farm. Their cover feature property, in our price range and area, began its description "Little houses in the woods..." so I looked at all the pictures. I loved this property, but the pictures did not seem to fit together. Then I re-read the beginning and caught the plural on the "house" and thought, "Does this property really have two houses? And EIGHT acres?" I knew we needed to see this property! And from what we had seen in this price range, I knew this property was going to move quickly!

I called the listing agent, but being Friday night, he did not answer. I left an urgent message requesting to see that property the next day somewhere around 3:00 PM, hoping that would allow for our appointments tomorrow as well as the return trip. Then I tried calling my realtor, who likewise was unavailable (almost as if they had a life, or something). I left another urgent message for her explaining what I found and left the listing agent's information.

Then I hung up and prayed.

In the morning, we had not heard anything from anybody, and were going to be incommunicado with our phones. I did not know the reason, but neither of our phones could get a signal anywhere in Indiana except in the Chicagoland vicinity.

"Well, Lord, I guess we will leave it up to you; because, frankly, that is our only option right now!" I sent up a silent prayer.

We saw a few properties that day, but nothing that encouraged us in our search. Quite the contrary. It was even more depressing than the prior two days had been.

We still had heard nothing because our phones were not working and, frankly, pay phones are just not a "thing" anymore; there were none to be found. We decided to console ourselves with lunch at a 50s retro diner that Jen had taken us to in Clay City, Glory Days. From there, we decided we would just head home, disappointed at our first real jab at house-hunting.

While sitting at our table, it occurred to me that we passed a pay phone on the way in, so I asked our waitress if the pay phone worked. She said no, that was a prop; but if we needed to make a call, just use the restaurant's phone at the register.

"Oh, my word: there's hope!" I thought.

I grabbed all the phone numbers I thought I might need, called Jen (who of course was in the middle of her son's birthday party) and she informed me that she had received my message and had contacted one of her officemates to cover for her to show us the house. She gave me her name, and I called. That realtor had left some messages for us telling us that she had a 3:00 appointment for the showing, she was just waiting for me to confirm. So, I asked the obvious question: We are in Clay City: is that anywhere near Rosedale? Can we even get there in time?

Our new realtor was not familiar with either place, so she could not help with that answer.

Nor was she familiar with Rosedale itself, so we chose an arbitrary intersection and agreed to meet there. Out in the boonies, my GPS had issues; in towns, she was mostly well behaved and reliable, and this was one time I needed her to be reliable!

As we raced the clock to get to the rendezvous on time, the heavens opened, and a torrential rain spewed forth; I made some comment to the effect of we needed this like we needed a hole in the head. Savanna, ever vigilant, said, "But mom, this is what you wanted; you told me that ideally it would rain right before we looked at houses so you could determine if the roof leaked."

Hmmm. Yeah, I did, didn't I?

We pressed on in silence (panic?) through the storm, and soon I observed a peculiar sight; I waited to see if Savanna said anything. Soon she said, "Mommy? Do you see that?"

I told her that yes, I did, I was just waiting for her to confirm and come to the same conclusion I had.

My mother had a notorious love of cardinals. Her Christmas ornaments oftentimes incorporated them, and she had more than one year sent out cardinal-themed Christmas cards; she fed them, and she had binoculars to watch them at her feeder. When I was young, a baby cardinal fell out of its nest, and we "helped" the mama cardinal take care of it until was old enough to fly away, although she never strayed far from our house; we all loved them.

In addition to that, my brother had given my mom a bluebird necklace one year for Christmas. This was the only gift, to our knowledge, that my brother picked out and purchased on his own for her, and she cherished it. It meant so much to her she wore it often, so Savanna associated bluebirds with her Mema.

I am relating this because during this rainstorm, on the way to what we were hoping was going to be our dream house(s), our car was being "dive bombed" by both cardinals and bluebirds. But that was not quite accurate, it was gentler than that; it was more as though they were guiding us.

Although still overcast, the rain abated in time for us to arrive at out meeting place, and our substitute realtor arrived just as we did. We followed her out to the house(s), praying all the while that her GPS worked better than mine which, currently, had us floating at no location.

Solely by the grace of God, we arrived at precisely 3:00 PM. There were indeed two houses, and we went through "The Dollhouse" first. This would be Savanna's home if we bought the property, and it was an adorable Amish-built log cabin. Basically, all one room, with a bathroom located in the rear. The owner had milled his own lumber to panel the entire inside as well, which lent a truly warm and inviting atmosphere. We heartily approved of this, so I was waiting with bated breath to see the other house.

The Doll House

We got back in the cars and had to follow a winding gravel drive through the woods to see the other home. And I swear, just as the home appeared in my view, up on a hill, the sun broke out and created a halo effect around this home; a beautiful, stone home.

My Dream House (a.k.a. The Money Pit)

The inside was not quite as charming but considering the price in comparison to what we had seen so far, the fact that there were two residences and that we both loved our respective homes (although mine would eventually be dubbed, "The Money Pit"), we put in a bid, on the spot, full price, with a check for earnest money to let the owners know we were serious about the bid.

They accepted our bid the weekend before my mother's birthday in May, and we closed the weekend before my father's birthday in August; the significance of those dates did not escape our notice. We were in no hurry, anyway, and the owners were gracious enough to allow us full access to the property in the meantime.

We have never regretted our decision to purchase these homes; mine is now remodeled inside, and I am quite pleased with the outcome. I wake up to the majesty of the woods, knowing my daughter is close at hand, and watch our cardinals feed from the feeder every day. Lately, I have even seen bluebirds feeding there; they always seem to appear when we need to see them.

Love you, Mema & Baga. I know you both love this place as much as we do. I wish we could have enjoyed it together but thank you!

Our watchful angel

The Proposition

The summer before I left for college, I wanted to be a little more sociable than I had been previously in my life. My parents had other ideas; they felt I should get a job. I figured there would always be time for a job, but I would only be truly carefree for a limited time. I found what I thought to be the perfect compromise: a receptionist position that was only 2-1/2 hours per day, beginning at 2:30. I could still go out at night, sleep in the following day and (just barely) satisfy my parents wish of having a job! It was a receptionist position at a Kidney Dialysis Center, and it was located next door to a car dealership.

During this period in my life, I loved walking and walked almost everywhere I went. My friend Jackie also liked to walk, so it would not be unusual for me to walk from my house on the east side of my suburb to her house at the west edge of the adjoining suburb, two miles all told, to pick her up to *begin* our walk. We would walk and talk for a couple hours; I would walk her home, and then walk home myself. I loved the solitude, I loved the quiet, and I loved the dark. The exercise was not bad, either!

So, it was natural for me to walk to work, and as this was my "summer of social" I would oftentimes arrive early to allow myself time to fraternize with my coworkers before clocking in. It did not hurt that I had a crush on one of the Resident med students (ok, make that three) working there. As I said, it was my summer of social!

As I was walking to work one "morning", I happened to see two salesmen from the Cadillac dealership next door waiting at the light to cross the busy street. As this was what I needed to do, I waited there a bit behind them, when the older of the two salesmen noticed me and said, "Hi, Cindy!"

Now, you may not know this, but having been a blonde all my life I can confirm and am willing to confide a secret to you: *All blondes are named either Cindy or Sue—no exception.*

Knowing he was trying to get my attention and being by nature recalcitrant, I ignored him. This was when he became louder and asked, "Aren't you Cindy?"

"No, sir, I am not."

Now he pulled out the heavy artillery: his business card, but he held onto it for a while. He said, "I see you walking quite often around here, do you live in the area?" I told him no, I worked at the Kidney Center.

"Oh, under Bob (the center's administrator); I know him well."

What he did not know is that Bob had the reputation there of being one of the most outrageous womanizers in the place; this did not speak well for Mr. Caddie, in my humble opinion. He asked me what I did there, and I told him. Then he offered me his card. I could tell his friend was becoming amused watching as I tried not to take it, but Mr. Caddie insisted that he wanted to take me to lunch "or something," and pushed it into the palm of my hand.

I must have had a strange look on my face, because then he asked me, in all sincerity, if I was married or engaged or anything and I burst out laughing. While totally delighting his friend, it frustrated him. He looked at me and asked what the problem was, then, and I said, still laughing, "I'm seventeen."

His buddy burst forth a guffaw simultaneously to Mr. Caddie swiftly extracting the business card from my hand. The two of them quickly crossed the street; one amused, the other humbled.

I realized later: *I never even saw his name!*

The Re-homing of Bronson

J had been engaged to a man I met in college, and although I realized that I loved him more as a friend than a life partner, it took a while for him to accept my decision and to move on with his life. Eventually he did, found another love and married her.

This was good in my opinion; we had accumulated a menagerie of dogs during our time together, and I liked to visit them. I also enjoyed my time with him, just not as a romantic partner. While Jackie, his new love interest, was never rude to me or made me feel otherwise unwelcome, I got the impression that she would *prefer* I not be there. As I said, there was nothing on her part that ever made me think so, it was something I picked up on subconsciously, with no confirmation from either of them.

When they first began dating, I visited the dogs frequently. As their relationship strengthened and I felt her resistance to my visits grow, I reduced the frequency of my visits out of respect; but I still loved my dogs, especially the one who made herself unwelcome in my parent's home: Temba and I had a special bond that neither time nor absence could break.

The week of my 21st birthday, I received the news that during Temba's fourth pregnancy, she was shot and killed by a hunter poaching on their property. I was heartbroken, especially since nobody knew whether she had given birth, and Temba's body had disappeared. But, as she was the real reason for my visits, I ceased them to allow Jim and Jackie's relationship time to grow as it would.

By now, my family had adopted Bronson, Temba's son, and he had secured his place in the family. He was really my dad's dog at this point, although technically mine. Then we experienced a tragedy in the family; my cat, who was Bronson's little buddy, had been hit with a baseball bat and we ended up having to put her down. At the time, we did not realize how attached Bronson was to this little girl; but we all watched as he spent the next week missing her and searching everywhere he could for her.

When he finally realized she was no longer in the house, he began to escape the yard; the first time he had ever attempted that, and then he repeated it. I resolutely believe he was out looking to see where his little buddy went, but it was February in Chicago, and our retired 75-year-old next door neighbor returned him to us four days in a row. I told my parents I did not want to be responsible for Mr. Baker having a heart attack chasing down my dog in the snow, so we all agreed that I would search for an alternate residence for him.

I asked around for a while, but there were no takers for a 120-lb. lap dog. Eventually, I found a no-kill shelter in Hinsdale and put him on a waiting list for entry. I hung up the phone from that conversation and felt ill; there had to be a better option for him: he was such a great dog!

Then I remembered something my ex-fiancé had told me a long time ago; Bronson was from Temba's third litter, and the other puppies had been placed on farms near Jim. The farmers raved about the dogs they got from him and told him they were the best farm dogs they ever had. I thought it would be worth at least a phone call to keep him out of a shelter, even a no-kill one.

I called Jim and we caught up on each other's lives; he and Jackie had married, they had two kids, they were now in town; what was new with me? I had just gotten married, and we had bought a house we were working on in Oak Park, etc.

Finally, I explained why I was calling; I wanted to know if there was any possibility of him finding a home for Bronson. He told me he would ask around and let me know. The night before I was supposed to confirm to the shelter that Bronson was coming, Jim called and said he had a family who was interested. They lived on a farm, had kids and a Doberman buddy for Bronson. I was thrilled and told him I would bring him down that weekend. I would drop him off with Jim, who would then take him to the farm.

I was ecstatic that my goodbye to Bronson would not be done inside a shelter! I gave my parents the good news, and on Saturday I prepared Bronson and his "stuff" for travel; my last road trip with him, how sad.

When we got to Lincoln (IL), Jim met me outside and brought me in to introduce me to the kids and to say hi to Jackie. We went back outside for him to meet Bronson, and he was taken with Bronson himself. I found it difficult to stay there and chit chat, knowing this would be the last I would probably ever see of Bronson, but Jim liked to talk, so we did.

Eventually, he got around to the fact that I was now married, and he said that he was surprised I came down alone. On a hunch, I said, "Let's just say that I think David feels toward you about the same way Jackie feels toward me."

He jerked his head back as though I had slapped him, and he was visibly stunned. I guess that was supposed to be a well-kept secret. After being quiet for a moment and thinking, he reached over and gave me a huge embrace. He said, "I hope you have a good life; you deserve it."

"Same for you," I said.

Ah, suspicion confirmed!

The Rose

*M*y mom was not nearly the hard-core gardener that I was, but there were certain flowers she loved, and wanted to make sure she had around her.

One of them was the Tropicana Rose. Wherever she lived, she planted at least one Tropicana rose bush. That was her father's favorite, and she took special care to memorialize him in that way.

Their last house really had no garden per se, other than one small, ± 3-foot square, area in the back corner of their property. It was either not good soil or was infected with something; neither of us could make anything grow there. Even rhubarb, a rather hardy plant and one with which my mother never had an issue, would not cooperate in that space.

But she endeavored and dug through rock at the base of their house to plant her Tropicana rose! For the life of me, I have no clue how she got through. She planted that, along with her white iris, purple poppies and her Peace rose. She also lined her property with six lilac bushes, right outside her patio door, so she could enjoy them from her kitchen table.

All were special to her, but the Tropicana took precedence.

The roses she planted there absolutely thrived! They climbed up the bricks of the house and made a spectacular backsplash to the side yard. Iris and poppies in the spring, roses late spring through summer, and her "naked lady" lilies in late July/early August. They all gave her pleasure to see.

The year she died, she died right before the lilacs came into bloom. It was difficult that year to watch her lilacs bloom, knowing that she was not there to see them. Throughout the spring and into early summer, nearly four weeks, my aunt, Aunt Dee Dee, and I worked on my parents' home cleaning it out in order to list it. By this time, dad was safely ensconced in the only retirement village that would take him (ironically, arguably the best one) because of his G-tube, so it was safe to clean and paint, clear out clutter, and do all the 'normal things' to stage and sell a home.

I spent many nights burning the midnight oil in their home, and it was cathartic because I never really had a chance to grieve the loss of my mother. The situation went so quickly from shock to responsibility and action, and then a lot of hard work, that it was probably two months before I really had a good, cathartic cry over her loss. And even then, it was only in the shower.

Aunt Dee Dee and I spent a lot of time together during this period. She was like an angel sent from heaven for me; I never would have made it through this ordeal without her help and support. The two of us became punchy on more than one occasion after working ourselves into exhaustion. She had a lot of great ideas for staging the home and for its general clean up and disposal of household items.

Finally, at the end of May, it was time to officially put the house on the market. We had an appointment with a realtor to sign the paperwork and get things moving. The realtor had a couple of suggestions, which I followed within the next week or so, but the house was officially listed.

The price must have been right, because within two weeks, there were two offers simultaneously. One a cash offer, one contingent. We chose the cash offer with no contingencies. So, now we had another glut of work to un-stage and empty the house!

Once again, Aunt Dee Dee and I worked feverishly, and I became frustrated because there seemingly was nowhere to give donations of used items; most agencies I contacted wanted near-new or new items. I had my house on the market, too, so I did not want to be dragging things home with me; I could not believe some of the items that we threw out literally for lack of finding a place willing to accept a "used" donation!

Near the end of the purge, a couple of days prior to closing, I treated my aunt to two nights at one of the local hotels. We were coming down to the wire and clearing everything out including the furniture. I was going to stay for the closing, but she was going to head home. This was our final night, and I noticed that the Tropicana, naked up to now, had produced two blooms.

My mother's ashes had been scattered in the local scattering garden part of the cemetery, and I had picked up a routine of purchasing a rose at the florist and scattering the petals there for her. I told my aunt about this practice and told her about the two roses on my mother's rose bush. I mentioned to her I was going to take one to scatter and invited her to do the same.

After the closing, I dropped my father off at his new home and proceeded to the scatter garden with my mom's rose. I noticed there were petals from another Tropicana rose already scattered. That year, my mom got the last two blooms from her bush; she was now with her father, and her Father. What a special year for her!

Mema's Rose

The Service

Time seemed to spin around me. There was so much to do. Having a small family, just my parents, my brother, my daughter and me, and limited visits with extended family because, geographically, we were removed from them, I had never experienced death first-hand. And certainly, never within a small community.

My parents belonged to a church and, God bless them, those members were Johnny-on-the-spot. Without their help, and the guidance of my aunt, Aunt Dee Dee, I would have been lost, clueless, and totally bereft. They knew the hurt we were experiencing, and they knew how to guide us. People whose names I had never heard volunteered, coordinated efforts, pitched in and helped us.

After visiting with my mom for the last time, their home became too much for my daughter to endure. I had to agree. I had already realized that everywhere I looked, I saw Mema. And right now, with her sudden departure, that was overwhelming to me. My daughter wanted to get home, as she was in the process of finishing her Associates degree, and she had a test on Monday morning.

Even though I assured her that death was an appropriate excuse to miss a test, she told me how she felt about the house and that she could not handle being here right now. Having already drawn the same conclusion independently of her, I understood. I drove her home Sunday morning and returned Sunday evening. I planned to pick her up the following Friday for the memorial service, but another angel placed in my life, Paula, offered to bring her down mid-week, thus eliminating another full day of travel for me.

I knew there was a lot to do, I just was not sure what it was; as I said, Aunt Dee Dee stepped in. We had an appointment with the funeral home on Monday, and it was not until that time that I realized that my mother's life at this point was nothing more than a name on the tab of a file folder. What an odd thought; but I had a lot of those about then.

Apparently, my parents had visited the funeral home and made all their arrangements. They gave me a copy of her obituary, and it felt like it had so little to do with my mom that I was offended. There was nothing in it that was "my mom". It was cold, it was factual, it was boring.

And it was apparently what she wrote.

There was nothing in there about how she brought life to all projects, excitement to all outings, the absolute dedication and devotion she had to both her husband and her children, or the compassionate and loyal friend I knew her to be. The current obituary described a corpse; I retooled it to describe my mother.

I wrote about her devotion to God, and her family. I wrote about how she is safe now, in the arms of her Father. I brought her corpse to life, even if just for an instant, for one last time. And we all agreed that it was more fitting than the original obituary.

Then came all the stuff with which I was unfamiliar. I knew nothing of visitations, or receiving visitors or gifts, or anything else to do with the ritual of death; for me, it was on-the-job training. And it sucked. I would have given anything to remain ignorant of such rituals. And even though I was 'the baby' of the family, apparently, I was in charge.

My dad was incapable, my brother unwilling, and my daughter was still shell-shocked. Thank God for my aunt! (Have I said that before?) Even though she had to have been grieving the loss of her sister, she stepped up to the plate like no one's business; or maybe she is just bossy, but she led me through the whole process. Which was good because I was still numb.

We planned the memorial service for a week from her death. My parents wanted to be cremated, so that was not an issue. They had not planned for any kind of service, but under the circumstances, that was not acceptable. My dad wanted to keep it that way, but I explained that, for most people, this was going to be a jolt; they needed to have a chance to say goodbye, as sudden and unexpected as her death was.

Eventually, he relented, and we planned the service. It was to be simple, but a service, nonetheless.

At some point that week, I remember suddenly feeling a flood of love and comfort. It was as though I could feel an angel, or maybe even God Himself, reach out and wrap Himself around me to protect me. He knew I was hurting and confused, and I found myself so profoundly comforted by this that I was able to, in turn, comfort others who were as shocked by her death as I had been. And I suddenly felt OK about my mother's death for the first time.

It enabled me to reconcile my feelings of loss with the knowledge that she was where she was supposed to be, and that in that place, all was well for her. She had no more heart condition, no more knee problems, no more aches, or pains, no more maternal worries (and I know I had given her more than my fair share), no more caregiving responsibilities; nothing now but love, and peace.

Our friends and relatives arrived for the service, and all expressed the same sentiment: shock and disbelief. I was not surprised at that, as I was the one who had planned to move to Texas with her, after I sold my house, and after we figured out whether my father would be able to handle the move, provided he was still around. This was not the first time in my life that I felt God has a sense of humor. Or, if not humor, at least irony!

There was not much of the service that I remember other than appreciating how beautiful it was and realizing there would be no photographs, as the family photographer was no longer here: she was the one being memorialized. I did not think that one through. I do remember the flowers, which were minimal, were perfect. My daughter had painted a watercolor portrait of my mom, and that was the featured picture at the service. We had a nosegay made and put in the corner of that picture, with a coordinating arrangement at its base. We also had some family pictures, but the centerpiece was the watercolor.

During the service, I realized that my daughter had painted my mother turned away from us and looking back at us, as though she was on a journey, and was preparing the way for us. As this was her actual role in life, I wondered if it was Savanna's premonition, or a simple coincidence?

My poor Aunt Mickey, the one in hospice, felt horrible that she could not be there to comfort her baby brother or to attend the service that day. She kept asking my cousin if it "was time". She passed away after the service; I can only presume it was so that she could offer her condolences in person, and to be travel companions on their journeys.

See? Irony.

The Snake

J suppose you might say I was rather adventurous as a child; head-strong, opinionated and stubborn, I went where the wind blew me. Or, more accurately, where I thought the wind should have blown me. I went where I wanted, did what I wanted, explored the world and conquered my little piece of it on my own terms.

If something struck my fancy, I would study it. I was not exactly a 'girly-girl' but not quite a Tomboy either; I would just as soon be playing with my brother's cap guns and worms as dolls, but I did like a good game of dress up. As a matter of fact, I kind of thought there was something about dolls that was creepy, anyway.

When I was three, my grandparents moved to Tacoma, and we took a trip out west to visit. We traveled by train, three and a half of what probably seemed like the longest days in my mother's life to that point, but the only thing I really remember about the ride itself was fighting my brother for the right to sit in the front seat of the observa-tion car. The fact that there were two front seats, one on each side of the aisle, did not deter us from fighting. What can I say? Some truths are universal and consistent.

Once we got there, I do not even think it had been fifteen min-utes before I was out in the yard 'exploring'. I found something that intrigued me: this beautiful little black snake with two yellow stripes running down its back, slithering along the bottom of the wood fence. I watched it for a while, and finally my little fingers reached out and closed around its wriggling body.

"*I GOT IT!*" I thought to myself, excitedly.

Just as I was celebrating my find and hauling in my writhing little treasure to take a closer look, I heard the most blood-curdling scream I had ever heard in my life. I turned to follow the scream, and there in the window of my grandparent's home was my grandmother, looking much like Munch's *The Scream* looking back at me.

I was so startled and scared that I dropped my little treasure onto the ground. And then I heard it: my name was being called. And not just my first name, it was my first name, my middle name, AND my last name; all at once! I did not know exactly what I had done, but I knew – all three names – this was not good, not good at all. I was in BIG trouble!

So, I did what any self-respecting three-year-old child in trouble would do: I hid. I was in the garage, under the car, and waited to come out until I thought the coast was clear.

Eventually, I realized that I was not in trouble, and that they were now only looking for me to ensure I was OK. So, I came out of hiding. Since my grandparents had only recently moved out there, they were not familiar with the indigenous species of snakes and did not realize that I had a hold of a harmless little garter snake.

But to this day, whenever I see Edvard Munch's painting, I think of my grandmother. And a snake.

The Sock Hop

J had my driver's license!

This opened an entirely new world to me, as it does for most 16-year-olds. At least, it did for those of my generation and prior.

It was freedom! It was a step into adulthood! It was like finally riding a bike without training wheels! I was in love with driving, and with the freedom that it engendered! But I knew nothing about cars which, in retrospect, I would have been smart to at least have learned the fundamental ABCs of maintenance.

I did not. I just figured I would do that before I bought my *own* car. In the meantime, I relegated the responsibility of maintenance to my parents, and took my place behind the wheel!

One Saturday night, and totally out of character for us, my best friend Sara and I decided to attend the Sock Hop at the high school. Neither one of us particularly liked dances, neither one of us particularly liked any guys at that time; we were just into the whole 50s retro craze thing predominating the school at that time. Our high school had a native-born 50's band, Jade, that had been somewhat successful on the tour circuit and was to play at the sock hop that night. We wanted to be there, having never heard them in person.

I grabbed the family car and trekked off to pick her up. I should add that this car was currently eight years old and had so far survived two teenage drivers. At least, most of it had. It was a Chevy 7-cylinder wagon. As I said, I do not know anything about cars (still!), but I do know it used to be an 8-cylinder car! The point being that it was not a new car, and there were issues. Issues with which I did not want to involve myself, nor to which was I privy.

When I got to Sara's house, having learned etiquette in a civil society from my parents, I parked the car and walked to the door to pick her up, rather than to sit outside and blare my horn for the world to hear. I never did appreciate that approach, but most teens did just that. As a matter of principle, I never left my house to a car honk; if you did not care enough to get off your duff and pick me up courteously, I did not need to be with you. I know that is a dying, if not already dead, sentiment, but that is how I felt at the time. Sara answered the door, and we immediately headed for the car.

I had noticed when I first started the car that it hesitated between the time I put the car in drive and the time I felt the car engage the gear. But that was, like, 15 minutes ago, and I had already forgotten that; we were off to a dance!

I turned on the ignition, then simultaneously put the car in drive and gassed it.

Oops! The car was *NOT* happy about that!

As a matter of fact, I heard a big "*BOOM*", and then a grinding sound on the pavement.

"SARA – RUN!!!!!!!" I yelled, as I evacuated the car. She did likewise, and we met behind the closest tree we could find, peeking around it on opposite sides to see what would happen.

Nothing. The car was suspiciously quiet now.

Deciding that the car, indeed, was not going to explode, we emerged from our shelter, and cautiously crept forward. We looked under the car and found – something – hanging down from the bottom. We did not know what we saw, but we did know that it was not normal. We went to get her brother, who was taking auto mechanics courses, to see if he knew what happened.

Turns out it was the drive shaft, lying on the ground. Which pretty much rendered the car immobile. Hmmm. I guess we are not going to the sock hop. And my parents, who NEVER went out, were at a party. Figures! They finally get a social life, and I had to call them at their party to come rescue us and their car.

Remember, this is not like today – my cell phone calling directly to their cell phone. Oh, no! This was in the olden days, where I had to go inside Sara's house to their landline phone, look up the phone number in the phone book (kept conveniently on a table near the phone in almost every house I had ever seen), call the host of the party to explain my predicament to have them interrupt the party to locate one or the other of my parents and get them on the other end of the line. It was "a process"; there was no such thing as direct or immediate!

So, I made the call and soon my dad was on the other end of the line. I tearfully told him what had happened and how we had escaped with our lives, but I believed I had dropped the drive shaft.

"Where are you?" he asked.

"At Sara's." I said.

"OK, I'll come and get you." He hung up.

"Really? 'I'll come and get you'? That's it?" I thought.

When he arrived, he asked if we wanted him to drop us off at the sock hop, but Sara and I looked at each other and realized our desire to go to the dance was pretty much over. I think, our desire to do pretty much anything that night was over.

She stayed at her house, and my dad drove me home. Then he returned to his party.

It was not until later, years later, I discovered that he had been fully aware that the U-joint was worn, and that eventually what happened to me was going to happen, regardless of who was driving; it was only a matter of time.

Gosh! It really would have been nice to know at the time that I had not done anything wrong. Or maybe that was partial payback? Just sayin'.

The Sunday Morning Incident

Jt was a beautiful day and a perfect day for my annual excursion to the nursery!

Today, I was going to reward myself with all the cute little baby plants I would need to fill my garden beds with color for the summer and into the fall. I had spent all of Saturday preparing the beds, and today was the prize for yesterday's hard work. Today I would choose and then plant all my little gardens: I could not wait!

I did one last quick look-around to ensure all was well and that all the little beds were perfect; weeded, roto-tilled and ready to go!

I got in the car, looking forward to my hour-long trip to my favorite nursery. I chose this nursery specifically because it is an extensive nursery, with much from which to choose, but also the route I opted to follow entailed driving on a winding road through the woods, a rarity in the Chicago area, and it was a beautiful drive. It was a journey I took once a year, and one I relished every time!

I headed out, and one of the first things I encountered was a big, black truck. He was in my lane on a little two-lane road, but he was stopped at the red light with his left turn signal on. I pulled to his right, technically in the parking lane, but I figured he would not care too much, as he was turning.

The light changed, and I gassed the car, heading straight. *Wait: so did he!* Oh, my! I was heading straight toward a parked car, so I 'put the hammer down' and pulled in front of him, returning to the official lane. And boy, was he *mad!*

He began tailgating me, honking the horn and being generally belligerent and annoying. I was really outraged that he would intrude on my beautiful day in such an ignorant manner and attempt to ruin it. Not to mention the people who might be trying to sleep in on a Sunday morning! As a matter of fact, he became SO annoying, I resolved to do something about it.

I stopped, in the middle of the road. And, since he was tailgating, he had no choice but to stop also.

I proceeded to get out of my car and approach his. I know, *stupid.* What can I say? I was caught up in the moment.

He rolled his window down and began yelling at me about how dare I pass him on the right by using the parking lane to get in front of him, blah, blah, blah. I let him yell for a while, because I wanted him to vent so that he could feel better.

When it seemed he was done, I apologized to him.

I told him he was right; I <u>did</u> pass him using the parking lane. And I told him I was deeply sorry.

I was sorry that I *believed* him as he sat in the left lane signaling a turn; and I was sorry for assuming that he would follow through; I told him that, should I ever see him in the future, I will know him to be a liar, and I will know better than to believe him. But for right now, the only error I made was in my decision to believe him.

He began to argue with me about his left turn signal, when I pointed out to him that it was, indeed, *still blinking.* He looked down at his dashboard and realized I was correct, although he was <u>never</u> going to admit it to me. He *wanted* to continue to argue, but realized he had no argument to make. I could see he was eating crow in his head right about then, and I loved the chastened look on his face.

I am not entirely sure he felt better; but I know I did. I happily resumed my annual excursion!

The Taste of Armageddon

I have a complicated relationship with my GPS. I call her 'my lady', and I realized how much she kept me company on road trips after she "died" upon reaching my destination, and during the 3-1/2-hour trip back I realized how lonely I was. So much so that as soon as I got back, I ordered a new one, exactly like her; my first taste of AI dependency!

When I got the new one, I took a trip to Indianapolis. I was campaigning for my candidate, the first time ever for me, but it was an important election. And as it turned out, that was the leg of his primary he conceded defeat, but that is a different story.

This story revolves around my return trip, a four-hour jaunt through Indiana and back into Illinois. I knew from both the time of day as well as season that this was *not* the time to venture into "Eisenhower expressway" territory. Not only would I be arriving at a bad time of day to drive on it, but it was also under construction in the vicinity of the loop, so I did not want to venture anywhere near there.

I decided rather than fight her authority, I would give myself over entirely to my lady; whatever direction she gave, I would follow, as long as she avoided the Eisenhower.

I was on 294 and I knew (because she had told me) that in three point some odd miles, I was supposed to veer right to head toward "Chicago". That was in the back of my mind, but I was distracted; so, when I saw the next "Chicago" exit (almost immediately after hearing that it was three point some odd miles away), I took it.

And I was rewarded with that obnoxious "RECALCULATING" notification that I seem to hear so often in my car. "Recalculating? You told me to veer right to Chicago!" I yelled at her. And then I remembered; it was to have been in three miles; funny what you realize all too late.

But, I figured, I am here now, I may as well ride this out; I was discovering new territory, anyway.

I followed directions into this labyrinth spaghetti bowl of roads and highways, and became utterly disoriented, other than seeing Chicago in the distance and knowing that was where I ultimately wanted to be; I just could not seem to get there from here!

I swear I followed her circuitous route unfailingly, but on a Sunday morning I was lost somewhere in the industrial part of Gary, Indiana, and I did not think this was anywhere I really wanted to be. Looking around at the desolation and desertion, I would say it seemed like it was nowhere anybody wanted to be.

But she was still giving me instructions to carry on, move forward, and I even got stuck, seemingly in a parking lot of a closed-down warehouse, waiting for a freight train to pass. Not very comfortable, especially as I was not the only car waiting. That was both comforting, and disconcerting.

Eventually the freighter passed, and she had me turn left, furthering my progress into the parking lot, it would seem, and then she told me to take the ramp just beyond the overpass to the expressway.

Ramp? To an expressway? I saw neither. Until finally, hidden underneath an overpass, I found the secret entrance ramp! I followed it, even though it had a "Road Closed" barrier carelessly tossed to the side but did not extend across the ramp, and that brought me to a six-lane highway.

A six-lane highway upon which nobody was traveling, and I mean NOBODY, but me.

How odd it felt to be entirely alone on a six-lane highway; so much so that I kept waiting for barriers to appear alerting me this route was closed. Even though it was almost noon, the morning was misty and foggy; I was praying for approaching headlights to indicate to me that I was not totally alone on this super-highway to nowhere. I traveled mile after mile, longing to see another car. It was creepy to feel so alone in a world of so many people!

And I got to thinking, I would bet this is how it would feel after Armageddon: I was imagining 'Mad Max', and 'I, Robot' and 'Terminator' all rolled into one.

Then, I saw them: oncoming headlights! *Hallelujah!* I was not alone on this highway; it *must* lead somewhere!

Then I realized that the approaching headlights, although indeed oncoming, were located on a frontage road, not on this seemingly abandoned road.

So, I decided if this is my last look around, I may as well enjoy it!

I was on an elevated expressway, as I said, six lanes wide. Three unused lanes in each direction, save for me. I saw old warehouses and deserted buildings. There was really nothing else to see, being in the misty clouds as I was, and I anticipated each curve to reveal a huge chasm in the road where I would fall through because the road was damaged. Or missing. Or an alien spaceship was waiting to take me. Or all the above.

It was probably the first time in my life that I could compare to awaiting what I believed to be imminent death; that was the feeling I had: when suddenly you realize that you are, truly, alone. Life, or God, chose you for this. And the realization that life around you will go on, regardless of your demise, and that what happens to you right now is only important to you, and incidental to the rest of the world.

I thought of missed opportunities, even though I had recently begun to venture out into journeys I had never experienced, such as campaigning for a candidate in which I genuinely believed. Being from the Chicago area, any belief in our political system was always rather jaundiced, at best. But I had found good people for whom to campaign; people who believed the way I did. And I was sure there would be more to experience.

As my mind was beginning to accept the possibility that this misty, dark, desolate morning may be my last one on earth, I saw it.

THE EXIT!

It had only been about six miles, but it was absolutely the longest six miles I have ever driven in my life!

And then I realized that this exit was going to dump me into the exact spot I was trying to avoid in the first place. But you know what?

I realized I really did not care!

The Teacher

There are just times you gotta let it out!

I was in the 'experimental' math group in eighth grade; they were "testing to see if eighth graders were capable of learning algebra and calculus". One day, our eighth-grade math teacher assigned us homework which, as far as we were concerned, could have been and probably was written by extra-terrestrials in a drunken stupor. "A + B = C. What is the value of 'A'?" with a bunch of other nonsensical, foreign parameters.

I do not know; tell me what "B" and "C" are and I can easily tell you the value of "A"! Up to that point, we had been taught strictly addition, subtraction, multiplication and division; no alphabet in our math, no, siree, Bob! We were math purists!

Our teacher was, to put it delicately, a rather odd bird who had made the misfortunate calculation to teach at seventh and eighth grade levels without benefit of deodorant, mouth wash, toothpaste, toothbrush, shampoo, comb, or soap incorporated into his daily routine. Back then there was no air conditioning, either; just a bunch of preteens with big mouths, who made him the brunt of many prepubescent jokes. Sometimes near the beginning of summer, being in his class was close to torture, and even walking past his classroom could be as bad.

Bad hygiene aside, he chose to introduce us to algebra by handing out a homework assignment at the end of class; no explanations, no preliminaries, just *poof* learn algebra, by homework proxy, no less! I usually did the homework assignments at the end of class; however, realizing that this might take more than just a cursory glance, I took it home with me.

"*WHAT???? This makes no sense.*" I thought to myself.

The next day in math class, he asked if there were any questions. I do not think that there was anybody in the class whose hand was not raised.

OK, I am just the *daughter* of a teacher, but even I know that in such a situation, this is where you stop the class, go back to basics and *teach*, without calling on <u>anybody</u>.

But he called on Kathy.

Now, I was not particularly a friend of Kathy's, nor was I necessarily fond of her; she was in with the popular kids. I was, well, not! But she did ask "the question" we all wanted to ask. And his response to her was, "That is such a Mickey Mouse question, I'm not going to bother to answer it. Any other questions?"

There are just times when I see an injustice done, and my emotions take over. Roiling under my calm demeanor was an emotionally-charged warrior for justice waiting to be unleashed, back when justice warriors fought for equality and not equity of outcome. I think we both realized, too late, that I was the only one with a hand raised.

He called on me: his mistake.

I stood up, looked him in the eyes and said, "If you're not going to <u>teach</u> the class, could you sit down and shut up so that maybe we could try reading it to understand?" I shot my mouth off, and then sat down with a huff in self-righteous fury: my mistake.

Very quickly, I realized, "*Oh My Gosh: it's Wednesday. He bowls with my parents tonight!*"

All he did was ask if there were any more questions, and I know you will be shocked to hear that no one else had any.

My parents left for bowling the same time as always; but I dreaded seeing their car returning that night and watched for their headlights coming down the alley. I saw them pull the car into the garage and then I turned my bedroom light off and jumped in my bed, feigning sleep. They came into the house, and then upstairs.

And...*nothing*.

For the next two weeks (at least), my parents reaped the benefit of the best behavior I have probably ever exhibited. When they came home that night from bowling and there were no fireworks, I became suspicious of their strategy. But, as time wore on and nothing came of it, I gradually relaxed again.

It took fully twenty years before I asked my dad if my teacher ever said a word to them about anything that happened in class. My dad said no, then asked what I was talking about. I told him the story, and he immediately said, "Yeah, but he was a jerk."

I told him that may be the case but reminded him that at the time he would have pointed out to me that I had been openly disrespectful to my teacher in front of the whole class, and that he would have sided with him.

"Yeah," he said, "you're probably right."

Probably? I know I am! But he *was* a jerk!

The Temper Tantrum

J t is difficult to maintain a friendship when the romance is over, even if there is motivation to do so. I had been involved with a man my freshman/sophomore year of college; Jim was two years' my senior and graduated after my sophomore year. He moved away after having received and accepted an offer of employment and by this time, we were engaged. He was living only an hour away from campus, and neither of us expected any complications from this arrangement.

During our relationship, we had amassed four dogs: his German Shephard and Great Pyrenees, and my Irish Setter and Alaskan Malamute. We both loved all of them, and initially, weekends were spent at his place exploring the area in which we were going to live. Near the end of my sophomore year, I made the decision to leave college, as the wedding was to take place mid-semester that fall, and inconvenient for a commute. We had planned it for October 27th, shortly after my 20th birthday.

This is what I told people anyway, specifically my parents; but really, I just wanted out of academia. Apparently, the group of high school friends I had felt more passionately about intellectual curiosity than all the people I had met in college put together. I missed engaging in philosophical discussions and debates as entertainment, and yet nothing in college came close to stimulating me as much intellectually. In truth, I was jaded regarding my college experience, and I wanted out.

I broke the news to my parents and my professors, all of whom expressed disappointment to some degree; my art professor chose that occasion to let me know that he had nominated me for a grant, which I had received for the upcoming year. I thanked him for the opportunity but asked that it be redirected to someone who needed it, as I would not be staying. I am not sure exactly what I felt at this time in my life, but I did feel this environment was suffocating and toxic.

Having officially withdrawn, my parents informed me that funding would be cut off. While flabbergasted at its rapid removal, I determined to show them: I would get a job and begin my 'real' life!

Without a car, I sought to limit my job search to the immediate vicinity. I went down to the local Arby's and applied; I came home with a job, a full-time 'opener'. Since I was on the early shift, this left my afternoons/evenings free. I soon became bored and applied at a restaurant as a waitress; I was hired on the spot. Although neither position paid much, I had limited opportunity to go anywhere or do anything, as I was either working or had no transportation; as a result, my coffers were filling up!

During this time, I noticed a subtle shift in my attitude. I was only nineteen and was experiencing life on my own terms for the first time; and I realized I enjoyed it. There were firsts of all kinds that I was experiencing, simple ones. Paying my own way, for one; planning my own meals, going to the grocery to purchase the necessary items, then preparing and eating my own dinners; all of this was new to me, and it was opening doors in my mind. The prospect of now "locking myself in" for the rest of my life with one man was daunting; but the thought of losing him was worse.

I sought solace, or possibly just escape, in socializing at both of my jobs; I met so many people from so many different walks of life, and they were fascinating to get to know. I went disco roller skating with two new friends, Eric and Melody, and Melody and I began to spend a lot of time together. She was one of the assistant managers at Arby's and we were always doing something to the store; that Christmas, she and I decided to paint the huge arched front windows with sponges and tempera paint to create a "stained glass" window effect; the only things it created were problems when it came time to remove the paint, and a lot of very scratched windows from scraping. Not one of our best ideas (although they *were* pretty).

There was another assistant manager there, John, and he and I became friends. Knowing I had no car, he offered to run errands with me; that morphed into going out to dinner and spending more time together outside of work. I never removed my engagement ring, indeed we never even discussed it; and there was nothing physical going on between us. However, I suspected I was falling for the man; and I was trying to figure out if that would be possible, if I genuinely loved Jim. I spent a lot of time trying to noodle that one out. But mostly, I just tried not to think about it, and enjoyed spending time in the moments I had, with each of my friends.

Eventually, reality slapped me in the face; John had purchased a new home, and I offered to help him clean and paint before he moved in. We were working on his house one Saturday, but I was quiet all day. John did not mention it until he took me home that night, but as we were saying goodbye, he asked why I had been so quiet. I told him that I was just preoccupied, thinking about something. He asked about what, and I answered that my first bridal shower was the next day.

He almost exploded, and asked, "If your first bridal shower is tomorrow, what am I doing here tonight?"

"You see? That was exactly what I was thinking!" I answered. He left quickly after that, and I knew I had a lot of thinking to do; I was crashing head-on into a deadline. I had been deliberating this exact question now for months; ultimately, I decided that I was too young to marry. Jim may or may not be the right man, but I did know that I felt too young to make that decision with any certainty.

Now, I just had to convey that to everybody.

It was a long and lonely night, and the dawning day was not going to be any easier. The first call I placed was to Carol, who was hosting my shower. I had no sooner gotten the words out of my mouth when she cut me off because "she had a lot of calls to make" and told me she would call me later as she hung up on me.

Then my parents arrived. I honestly did not realize until I saw them how much of an emotional dilemma I had been in, but my logical and totally mature response in seeing my parents was to cry; and when I broke the news that I could not marry Jim, my mom hugged me and told me I could move home; that made me laugh! She obviously did not get it: *no, mom, I need to grow up!*

Bottom line, the wedding was called off; John and I began officially dating, but Jim was not giving up easily. I tried hard to keep things friendly between us – after all, I did not want to give up visitation rights to any of our dogs – but he was making it more and more difficult to be friendly, or even nice.

After some time apart, Jim and I were able to talk, and I told him I still wanted to keep in contact with him and see the dogs occasionally. He agreed, and we set a date for a visit, that following weekend.

He was happy that I came to see him again; he took me out to dinner, we took the dogs to a park, he had moved and gave me a tour of his new place. As the visit progressed, he told me that his sister and brother-in-law were throwing a party, and he invited me to be his guest. I asked the date, and he said, "October 27th".

I said, "Based simply on the date, I would have to say no."

"Buy why?" he asked. I explained that the date of our called off wedding was probably not the optimal time for us to be showing up at a party together; he claimed that did not matter, but I held fast, realizing that a friendship with this man may be out of his comfort level. Indeed, I still had not told him about John; but I was honestly impressed with the progress that he *had* made, and I was concerned that news would make him regress.

I went home, and again distanced myself for a while. My birthday came, and a dozen red roses appeared at my door. They were from Jim, and the card asked me once again to accompany him to the party. I was so angry with him that I threw the roses away; I called him and told him for the last time, that date is not appropriate for us to see each other. Period.

Saturday the 27th rolled around, and John and I spent the day working on his house. By this time, he had moved in but was doing some remodeling, and I was happy to help. He drove me home about 10:00 because we were both tired; he came in to have a scotch and talk for a bit before he left.

Someone pulled in the driveway, a semi-circular gravel drive that ran around the apartment building, and for whatever reason, I looked out to see who it was.

I turned to John and asked, "Well, are you ready to meet him?"

"You're kidding, right?"

"Nope: he's here."

John tried to leave inconspicuously to allow me some private time with Jim; he was aware of Jim's invitation and knew my feelings on the matter. However, there was only one way in and one way out of my building, and the two met at the doorway. From Jim's reaction, I think that was the first time he might have suspected "another man," even though we had been broken up now for months.

I did introduce the two, but John swiftly disappeared; I invited Jim in to talk.

I quickly realized that talking was beyond his capability at this point; not only was he angry from running into John, but he had obviously "imbibed" prior to his arrival, and even without the anger was probably incapable of any serious talk.

He vented his anger a bit, then told me he was leaving; because of his condition, I followed him to his car and found out that his friend, Sewer (Mike), was with him. Out of Jim's earshot, I asked how much Jim had to drink, but I think Mike was covering for him; he told me not much. While I was talking to Mike, I was also petting Lucky, the German Shepherd, who was in the back seat. Jim lashed out at me and yelled that I was not to touch "his dog." I backed away from her, held both my hands in the air and asked, "Fine; am I allowed to speak with *your* friend?"

"You can speak with my friend but leave my dog alone!" I just looked at Mike and whispered, "Take care of him, please."

With that, Jim got in the car and gunned the accelerator to leave; the driveway, being gravel, caused the car to lose purchase in its curve, and he hit the corner of the garage abutting the property. Rather than stopping, he drove away; I could not believe he would do that!

As I headed back to my apartment, someone approached me from the front yard: John had not left; he had remained to ensure my safety. I told him what had happened with the garage, and we decided a walk in the fresh air would do us both some good. As we walked down the block, a cop car arrived and parked on my street; a huge cop emerged from its interior. Before I knew what was happening, John said to the cop, "You are surely an ugly MF-er!" (although he did not abbreviate).

I seriously thought, between John and Jim, they were determined to kill me that night! But then John continued, "How ya doin', Bear?"

That big ole cop chuckled, and the two embraced; I found out they were good friends (thank God!). John asked what Bear was doing there, and he said that somebody had set off the silent alarm on a garage in back; he was there to check it out. It turns out that the appliance store down the street rented that garage to house extra stock, and they wired an alarm directly to the police station.

John explained to Bear what was going on, and about that time, Jim came back. I was so happy that he decided to do the right thing!

266

When he got out of the car, Bear approached him, and said, "I heard that garage back there jumped out in front of you." With that, I was confident that things were calm, and under control, and John and I headed back to my apartment.

Jim and I did not see each other for quite a while. When we did speak again, he thanked me for holding fast and standing my ground, because he admitted he tried to bully me back into our relationship. However, after he accepted that I had moved on, he met the woman he would later marry. I was happy for them both; mostly, I was happy that I could still visit my puppies; he had once again opened that door to me.

The Vacation

The first time I thought of taking a vacation independently of my parents was when I was twenty. I had started my first real full-time job, and our company had twelve ancillary offices throughout the states, and one in Canada. The national headquarters was in Ft. Lauderdale, and I had never been to Florida.

My job as the receptionist was to answer phones and direct visitors to the proper people; but also, and probably because I got bored, I augmented the collections department: I have always done good phone. I made collection calls and updated the Florida office on fiscal progress made with our customers.

I spoke daily to the General Manager, John, of the Florida office, who headed up collections, and he became one of the highlights of my day. We communicated by telephone and TWX (I know – most of you are out there saying "I think she misspelled something – what is a TWX?"), which really did exist and was fascinating; it was a precursor to the fax machine, and quite advanced, for its time.

For months we telephoned and TWX-ed, and we became friends. I reiterate, I was twenty. I did not know how old John was, but I did know he was significantly older than that. And he was married. And although I enjoyed talking with him, there was never anything untoward in our relationship; certainly not on my side, and nothing of which I was ever aware from him; he was always a gentleman.

One of the young salesmen from Ft. Lauderdale, Keith, visited our office in July. Keith was young and unique in his looks; not quite handsome, but he would certainly catch your eye. At least, he did mine, and he asked me out, which I accepted.

We had a wonderful time. He took me to one of the nicest restaurants in my hometown, and we talked throughout the entire dinner. He described what living in Florida was like and told me about a crab shack close to his house that was one of his favorites. Eventually, we moved to the bar to continue our date. It was a piano bar, and we enjoyed joining in to sing the 'ole time' songs they were playing.

During this evening, Keith invited me to visit him in Florida. He promised to take me to this crab shack, and to put me up for the duration. Although I initially thought he was kidding, it did plant a seed.

My vacation plans began formulating...I had a free place to stay, and I could drive there. What else do you need? (Oh, I was so incredibly young, and had so much to learn!)

After a week or so, I called Keith and asked if he was serious about the place to stay, if I visited. He was excited about the prospect and said that of course he was serious. So, it was just a matter of hammering out the details, and letting my company know when I was going to be gone.

John was also happy to hear that I was coming down for a visit, and although I was never entirely convinced that he cared much for Keith, he never said anything directly to me. I just got that impression.

The next big hurdle was to 'break the news' to my parents. My dad was cool with it, but my mom's reaction was, "There's no way a twenty-year-old kid should be driving alone across the country! No, you can't go!"

I remember my dad took her by the elbow and turned her to him and said softly but firmly, "Twenty-year-old *young lady*. She's an adult, and if she wants to, she can go."

Yay, dad!

So, having jumped all hurdles, the trip was on! I even coordinated with my friend, Jackie, to drop her off in Cincinnati to visit Henry, her boyfriend, on the way down. This made my mother happy knowing I would have company for at least half of the first leg.

I must digress for a moment, for those of you who did not live in this time, to tell you some of the facts of life back then. There were no ATMs. There were few, if any, national banks, and no credit cards, at least, no major cards, and certainly not for someone of my age. You had to first develop a credit history, and then once you proved you were credit-worthy, you could be 'trusted' with a credit card. (Backward philosophy for today's easy credit, but in my humble opinion, the correct one.)

In my (limited) financial bracket, there was only one real option: checks or cash. There were traveler's checks of course, but I was already on a shoe-string budget, and even that nominal fee was out of the question.

So, planning a vacation like this became a little more involved because contingencies needed to be anticipated (and remember, I had never even been on vacation without my parents; I had no idea what to expect). Reluctantly I took about $100 cash for incidentals; back then, not only was that a lot of money, but traveling with that amount of money was risky: if you lost it, you were just out of luck. I figured should I need more, I could visit a local bank and cash a check.

The very last thing I did, the night before we left, was to call Keith to confirm his offer and to let him know that tomorrow was the day we were leaving Chicago. I had been getting some strange vibes from him as the planning progressed, but he asserted that everything was fine and that he was still expecting me.

So off we went, Jackie and I, to drop her in Cincinnati, which impressed me as a beautiful city. We drove into the city at dusk and were rewarded with a stunning sunset view of the city reflected on the water. What water, I did not know. But it was gorgeous! After I dropped Jackie off with Henry, I continued, to see where I would land that night

I was so excited to begin my Floridian vacation that I drove straight through! I arrived in the Ft. Lauderdale area at about 1:15 AM. And, although I found his house, Keith did not answer his doorbell. And realize, back then there were no cell phones, either. If you wanted to place a call, you had to (1) find a pay phone; (2) get out of the car, and (3) pay upfront for the call, *with change.*

Assuming him to be a sound sleeper, I decided to get a room for the night; I had allowed for an overnight stay on the ride down anyway, so I could try him again in the morning when I had access to the phone in my room. For now, it had been a long day that was beginning to catch up to me; I needed to rest.

I touched base with Keith in the morning, Sunday, although it took me a while to reach him. I got the impression that he was surprised I was there, even though his was the last call I made prior to leaving. We planned to meet at his house at a certain time, and we got off the phone.

When the time came, I drove to his house and got one of the chilliest receptions I have ever received. It was stilted from the get-go. He showed me to 'my' room (his bedroom), and then made a big show of letting me know he would be sleeping on the couch. [*OK, I was not really expecting to sleep with you, but glad you clarified that.*] I told him that, as his houseguest, I would be happy to sleep on the couch, and probably more comfortable there then kicking him out of his bed, but he insisted I take his bedroom.

Once I got settled, we watched Night of the Living Dead. It became apparent to me quickly that I had become a burden to be endured and endured simply because he had made an offer to me months ago; he was just too wimpy to tell me when I called to confirm that things had changed. You know, when I called from home where I could have accessed resources if I needed them, rather than being stuck in Florida with no money. Or parents. Or even, apparently, friends!

I could only surmise that somewhere in the equation was a newly minted girlfriend, unhappy (and probably surprised) with my arrival. I think that, even though I called him specifically to confirm, he really did not believe I was coming. My first real-life lesson on communication between the sexes. *Yay, me: I am out there in the world, amassing practical knowledge!*

I did some mental calculations as we watched the movie and figured that I would need to stay three or four nights. At that point, I would have sufficient funds to stay at a motel, if I watched my spending. I told Keith what I was thinking, and initially he tried to tell me I was wrong, that I was welcome to stay; but I do not think even he believed what he said. Eventually, although he pretended to be insulted that I was planning to leave, there was also an element of relief in his demeanor. And he insisted that he still take me to that crab shack, since he had promised to do so.

And that was really the impression I got; that he was *going* to follow through only because he promised, not because it was something that he wanted to do. Just like 'allowing' me to stay in his home, because he promised, not because he wanted to. And, although I tried to let him off the hook, he was insistent, and we decided to go Thursday to that crab shack; the same day I figured I could realistically leave for a motel, and reprieve.

On Monday morning, Keith left for work and showed me where the extra key was kept outside his house in case I wanted to leave and lock up/get back in. I had already made lunch plans with John, so I started getting ready for that.

We had a nice lunch; John was a genuinely nice man, and again, I never felt there was anything other than friendship between us. It was during this luncheon that he confirmed my impression he did not care for Keith, and he told me that I could call him if I needed anything.

Our lunch was terrific, and he even took me back to the office to meet some of the other people with whom I had occasion to speak. We had a good visit there, and John wanted to get together with me again later in the week for either lunch or dinner; I was staying about eight or nine days, and since I was driving, I really did not have a hard and fast departure date. I told him I would have to see how the rest of the week panned out, but that I would like that.

On Tuesday, I decided to visit the beach. I hate 'sunbathing' or even being on the beach (not a fan of either the sun or the sand), but it was so uncomfortable in the house that I did anything I could do to get out of the house, returning only to sleep.

At the beach, I met Bob. He tried to teach me to body surf and it was fun, if not entirely successful! We carried that over to a diner and spent the balance of the day together. When he heard the unfortunate circumstances of my 'accommodations' he offered to let me stay with him for the rest of the time I was there. I thanked him and told him that, although I appreciated the offer, I had learned my lesson. And I was not about to jump from the frying pan straight into the fire. I would just stick to Plan B of moving on Thursday, after the crab shack dinner. Then he invited me out on a date after the crab shack dinner, which I accepted.

I wondered how I was going to broach the subject with Keith of having a date immediately following our 'date' on Thursday, but I figured I would cross that bridge later, as I had enough on my plate with him at this time. I did not want to hurt him, but I could not fathom why he had not spoken up before I left Chicago; I was kind of enjoying this situation, as I was feeling simultaneously stung and stuck.

I spent Wednesday wandering around, but I was very dispirited with this vacation. I seemed to be spending my time thinking of ways to stay out of his house. I challenged myself to go to a movie by myself, also a first, and saw *Only When I Laugh*. How appropriate! I wandered alone (and fascinated!) through boutiques and malls. For those of you who do not know, malls were a new concept at the time. And boutique malls? Well, we just did not have any of those back home! It did keep me occupied for a large portion of the day.

When I got hungry, I decided to go to an Arby's that I had seen. I worked at an Arby's in my college days, so it felt comforting in a bizarre way. And when I walked in, I saw they even had my all-time favorite video game, Galaxian, sitting in the corner; now I really felt at home!

I ate my dinner, then headed over to the game and I played, and played, and played. Eventually, I realized I had an audience, the Manager, Jay. My first thought was that he was going to kick me out for having been there so long; but he had been watching me play and asked if I wanted to play against him, which of course I did. He was good, and we ended up playing for hours! It came time for me to go, and he asked if he could see me again.

I had not really looked at him until then (I took my Galaxian play *very* seriously!), and I realized he was quite handsome! But when I said sure, and we tried coordinating our schedules, we discovered that we had only Saturday night for our first date because of previous engagements, mostly mine. [Believe me – this was a standalone event in my life!] And I was planning to leave Sunday. Well, so be it, then: we would have our first date on Saturday!

I think that was about the first time I really looked forward to something on that vacation. In the meantime, I had to go back to Keith's house. One more night and I could afford to venture out on my own. You have no idea how much I was looking forward to that!

Do not get me wrong; I really did enjoy my vacation, away from the house. I had never been to Florida, and there was so much to do and see that was vastly different from Chicago, and everything seemed so exotic just because of the setting. It was exciting to explore but staying in a place where I basically felt like an intrusive burden took a toll on my enthusiasm; I was very much looking forward to my Floridian independence!

Thursday morning arrived, and I was thrilled looking forward to my after-date date. I had one more dinner to endure, the 'obligatory' date, and then I would be free! I still had not told Keith that I had a date at 8:00. I know it was terrible, but I was trying not to even see him, let alone speak with him.

That morning when I saw Keith, he told me that he needed to make it an early dinner, because he had to be home by 8:00 for his date. Ha! He just handed me an opening on a silver platter! I told him that worked out perfectly, as it would allow me to be here for <u>my</u> 8:00 date. The look he gave me told me he did not believe me and thought that I was just trying to save face, but he did not really know what to say.

He got back from work early, and we proceeded to the crab shack; and believe me, it was not worth all the hype he had given it. It was a crab shack. And it was obvious that neither one of us was enjoying the company; both of us adopted the "OK, hurry up, order and eat. The sooner we do, the sooner we can get the heck out of here" frame of mind. For the record: he promised me this meal, and he provided it; it was one fine dining experience I will never forget, no matter how hard I try. And I do try!

It was too bad that this would be our last evening together, and that this would be our final impression of each other, because there was no way I was intending to contact him again, and I am sure, he felt the same. But we really had hit it off so well during the summer, and he really was a nice guy, just apparently very wimpy.

We got home at 7:30ish; plenty of time for our respective dates to arrive. I know that Keith doubted me, except my date arrived first. I had my car pre-packed, and I was ready to follow Bob as soon as he appeared so that I could check into the motel I had called; he was going lead me to it.

I never did meet the newly minted girlfriend, as she was not there when I left. Too bad.

I had a nice time with Bob, but the whole time I was really thinking about Jay, the manager, and looking forward to Saturday night. I was extremely excited to see Jay again! Bob was a sweet guy, but I wanted to get to know Jay!

Bob dropped me off at my motel, and it was such a blessed relief! Thursday night, and I could relax, finally, on my vacation! I could watch what I wanted on the TV and not worry about being presentable or anything. But mostly, *I could BREATHE!!!!*

I bopped around on Friday and just enjoyed the day! I even sunbathed by the pool for a little while. I spent the evening at the motel, I was enjoying my freedom and solitude so much; but I knew Jay was working and I knew he got off late, 1:00 AM or so. I decided, since I was now my own woman and could come and go as I pleased, I would pay him a visit.

He was both flattered and surprised that I showed up, and after he dumped his closing on his Assistant Manager, we took off. I just enjoyed seeing the sights of Ft. Lauderdale through his eyes. I learned all about him; he was a misplaced New Yorker and had a roommate. He had been in Ft Lauderdale only a couple of years and had not really found anyone to his liking. He was still close with his family, especially his sister, but they were in New York, and he missed them. Of course, I assumed this was all BS for my benefit, but then, hey, I was on vacation, what did I care?

After a couple of hours of touring, he dropped me off at 'my place' and we finalized plans for tomorrow's (tonight's!) date; especially after this evening, I anticipated the evening even more! I still had a tentative 'date' with John, but I owed him a call. My dance card was full by now.

Late Saturday when I woke up, I called John basically just to bug off, because I did not know how I could go out this evening, meet John for brunch or lunch Sunday, and still have a decent departure time to begin the drive home. But John would not hear of that! He suggested breakfast instead, and we left it at that. I figured what they heck: who needed sleep, anyway?

Now to concentrate on tonight's date! Jay told me he was going to take me somewhere for which I needed to dress up a little bit. Not a problem; my working philosophy was to always be more dressed up than anyone else in the room, so I did have a supply of dressier attire with me. But I did not know where we were going.

He took me to Jai Alai: I had never even heard of it. It was exciting and we were betting arbitrary numbers. At one point, he asked me my birthdate so he could use those numbers to bet. We did not win, but it was a nice gesture!

After Jai Alai, he took me for a long walk on the beach, where there was this huge full moon hanging low over the water. Oh my gosh, I thought maybe I had died and was in heaven! Handsome man on my arm, walking barefoot through the sandy beach with nothing but gorgeous vista all around us. The theme from the movie *Arthur* to this day reminds me of that night. Something about getting caught between the moon and New York City...

So, we just hung out together, enjoying each other's company. At one point, we got in his car and went through the drive-through at 'his' Arby's. This was a definite retrofit to what we know as drive-throughs today. Though the speaker was on the driver's side, you had better have a passenger with you when you picked up your order, as the pick-up window was on the right side of the vehicle when you pulled up! The speaker for ordering was in a blind spot with no cameras, no mirrors, nothing to indicate who was ordering, so when Jay was asked what he wanted, his response was "A couple of doobies, a line, and a Coke." There was a pause, and the speaker quipped, "Well, I can help you with the first two items, but I don't know where in the he** you're gonna get a Coke!"

Obviously, his NY-infused voice had outed him to his employee!

We stopped in the lobby for a quick hello and a visit, and then went on our way. We ended up in my room (fully dressed, of course!) lying on the bed watching the *Three Stooges*. Boy, I knew I had it bad for him when I was watching *them*: I cannot stand the *Three Stooges*!

We lost track of time, and I was so regretting not having made time for him earlier in the week. I really wanted to get to know this man much better! And he was having a difficult time leaving, knowing that I was going back home the next day.

Eventually, I had to kick him out. I was so tired I caught myself nodding off a few times! But I realized, it was close to morning, and I had to get at least a couple of hours' sleep so I would be minimally coherent for my breakfast 'date' with John. And I needed time to get ready, as well. But Jay made me promise to go out to lunch with him after my breakfast date. It was an 'obligation' that I was happy to fulfill, so I accepted.

It was great to see John again, but I was overflowing with excitement from the previous night, and it showed. I updated him a bit on the whole Keith situation. He was happy that I had eventually found someone more appropriate with whom to spend my time. This gave me the perfect opening to explain to him that I had to cut our breakfast short so that I could spend some time with Jay and say a proper good-bye.

John took the hint, and we parted. It was good to meet him, and we had a great time together. But I really wanted more time with Jay!

We met at the restaurant because I had already checked out. It was so good to see him! We luxuriated in each other's company, and before we knew it, our lunch had stretched out to 4PM. He tried to get me to order dinner, but I told him that I absolutely *had* to leave; I knew I had to at least get out of the city and away from him, or I would never leave. And my dog was at home, not to mention my job.

He suggested that I stay a couple more days, and he would pay for my flight back. I reminded him that would be a little costly, as my car weighs a lot! But he told me I could leave it there with him, and he would drive it up to return it in about a month.

I told him I really could see me breaking *that* news to my parents:

> "Mom, dad, I met a guy in Florida. We did not get a chance to really know each other, so I stayed a couple of extra days and he paid for my flight home. My car? Oh, don't worry about my car; it's with him. He will drive it up about a month. In the meantime, do you think I could borrow yours? At least, until mine's returned."

Yeah, that was not going to happen!

He did, however, talk me into going back to his place to meet his roommate. I really liked his roommate, and the three of us had a great discussion for a while, but I knew if I did not leave, it would be dangerous for me. I had to get on the road. At this point in time, my goal was just to get out of the immediate vicinity of him and far enough away to make it inconvenient to get back easily, then get on the road early in the morning and drive straight through.

After a very emotional departure, especially considering how recently we had met, and promises to call and/or write (how old school!), I finally tore myself away. And that is exactly what it felt like!

I drove until I knew I could not anymore, which (as tired as I was) was not too long. I only drove a couple of hours north before I had to stop. I physically could not keep my eyes open anymore. But it was far enough away for me to realize that vacation was over. And after some sleep, I could head back home in the morning with a clearer head!

I did really enjoy my first vacation. I think more for the first strike at independence than anything else, but I also learned a lot about myself; I could see more vacations in my future.

And the best part? Jay continued to call; and I even received a birthday card *on my birthday*. He also told me that he named a pigeon nesting on his balcony after me, so "he could feel closer to me"; I am not sure how I felt about that, though.

I realized that being alone on a vacation allows for much flexibility. Some boredom, too, but life is, after all, a balancing act. I felt it had been a successful vacation, all in all, with the realization that when push comes to shove, I can rely on myself.

The Vet Med Program

It had been my lifelong dream to become a vet. At least, it became my dream after I realized I probably could not become a nurse, as I was too squeamish with blood. Why that did not translate into veterinarian issues, I am not sure, but I could do almost anything with animals without it affecting me physically; one of the mysteries of life, I suppose. Or maybe a stronger motivation.

This dream also surfaced after I realized I probably did not have the talent to be an 'Artiste', at least enough talent on which to survive. But I did have a true love for animals, all animals. Throughout my life, my menageries included tropical fish, underwater frogs, tadpoles/ frogs, mice (unbeknownst to my parents), guinea pigs, and rabbits. Eventually, I had my own dogs and cats, too. Each had its own story, and each had his or her own place in my heart.

The neighborhood considered me their 'on call' vacation caretaker for animals. I did not even really care if they paid me or brought anything back for me; I just loved animals, and the more I met, the more I wanted to meet.

I left for school, conveniently a college that had a vet med program, but without really knowing what I was going to 'do' with my life. I always hated that obligatory question asked by relatives and other 'well-meaning' adults: "What was I going to 'do' with my life when I grew up?" My answer seemed obvious to me: I was going to live it, of course, what else? However, this answer never seemed to satisfy them.

College made me realize why this question was so frequently asked, as focus became more relevant. However, I came of age pre-computer-into-computer age. And I had noticed that, as computers became more prevalent, 'common sense' seemingly lost ground.

For instance, most colleges began placing a huge emphasis on GPA, as well as ACT and SAT scores. Why? All that proves is that one can read and temporarily retain information: what about the practical application of knowledge? Did anybody care about that?

This was my predisposed mindset when I arrived at college; a little jaded perhaps, but my mindset, nonetheless. I was deliberating between liberal arts, leaning toward fine arts or the new curriculum 'Medical Arts' (which I never did understand; I envisioned kneecaps with smiley faces on drawn on them), or Vet Med.

I know: two vastly different curricula, but that was where I was heading. In the meantime, I enjoyed my freedom!

I met people, and for the most part, my high school friends were already gone, between being younger than me and still in high school or making a real break and attending out-of-state colleges. None were around anymore, apart from one who lived off-campus, and I did not have a car. So, I acquired a new circle of friends, based really on classes and proximity to my dorm.

One of the groups I began to run with had a huge assortment of people, all of whom used nick names; I do not know why. My friends became T-squared, Dogface, Sewer, Beaner, Freak Week (who was also known as 'Lurch', and if anyone is familiar with the old Adams Family on TV it was because he really did look like him), Ter a.k.a. Glenn, Juan (who, irrespective of his name, was Jewish, not Hispanic), Cowboy, Leo (a female), and so on. I am not sure I knew anybody by his or her real name, but that was not so important to us at the time; it was who they were that was important.

I began to date Beaner, and he lived with Lurch (Freak Week). I knew Lurch was in Vet Med, and I would occasionally ask about the curriculum; generally, I was impressed. However, there came a pivot point; a point in my life I knew I was going to veer off, and I even knew why that was.

I was leaving Beaner's house once and heard a strange noise. I looked across the street and saw, locked on the neighbor's enclosed porch, a kid, a baby goat. I knew the girls who lived in that house were in the Vet Med program with Lurch, and so I thought to myself: *"Self, take note: ask Lurch, 'Why?'"*

And the next time I saw Lurch, I did.

His answer was disconcerting. Keep in mind, there were (at the time) only 28 accredited Vet Med schools in the US, this being one of them. I knew, even in my ignorance of all things 'Vet Med', that in our state, vivisection on pregnant females was illegal. And though I had been raised in a suburb close to a huge urban area (Chicago), I knew what a pregnant goat looks like: they are about as wide as they are long.

He told me the goat assigned to these girls to practice surgical techniques was pregnant enough that when the girls cut her open and realized she was pregnant, the kid could be removed and was able to survive on its own; and it was determined the girls were allowed to keep the baby.

This meant that the goat was not just pregnant, but *well into* its pregnancy. Meaning it should not have been in the program in the first place; meaning the administrators responsible, or whomever, should have known better; and if they did not, the professors should have known better; and even barring that, *those Vet Med students should have known that goat did not belong in the program!*

But again, GPA, SAT, ACT: no accounting for common sense.

That was the day I lost faith in our collegiate system; that was the day I figured it was just a matter of time before I dropped out and started to live; that was the day I did not believe in my college anymore.

It was not a good day.

The Visit

This is going to be the most difficult chapter for me.

I received a call from my mom that Aunt Mickey, my father's only sibling, had been put into hospice. While that sounds bad, it was the third time that year I had received the same call, and it was only April. She lived in the same town as my parents, so it was an opportunity for me to visit them, as well. I generally visited them every other weekend anyway, but had been neglecting other filial duties, such as visiting my aunt.

The first time she was placed in hospice, my daughter and I were upset about it, and we immediately rushed down to say goodbye. I knew she had been in bad shape, but I had not seen her as often as I should have. We had a nice visit with her; actually, a couple of great visits throughout the weekend, and we went back home feeling as though we had said our goodbyes, and everything was as it should be.

Throughout the next couple of weeks, I kept tabs and she seemed to be improving. She improved so much, in fact, that she was released from the hospital, and eventually hospice care was likewise released, as they were no longer needed: great news!

Until we got the same call a few weeks later. Again, we headed down to pay our respects, appreciating the chance to spend some more time with her and to talk with her again. We spent the weekend visiting with her in the hospital and strengthening our love for her.

And she recuperated once more; although when they released her this time, they did say that it was just a matter of time.

I got the call in early April that she was once again placed in hospice. This time she had been moved to a hospice facility. "Okay, mom, I'll be there this weekend to see her." My daughter opted not go, as she had plans with some friends and was looking forward to seeing them. So off I went, once again, alone.

When I got to my parents' home, I could tell my mom had had 'one of those days'. She was the sole caretaker for my dad, who had Parkinson's, myasthenia gravis, prostate cancer, congestive heart failure and high blood pressure, among other things. It had been over 10 years, and each Christmas we assumed 'this would be his last'. Somehow, he kept trudging along, but its toll was becoming evident on my mom. That day, when I arrived, she seemed tired, and to want quiet; so, I obliged.

I made sure to go say hi to my dad, whose habit was to stay in the living room and watch the big TV while mom and I sat at the kitchen table and chatted. I gave him a hug and a kiss, asked how he was doing, and then joined my mom.

She had fallen asleep at the table, a frequent phenomenon, so I watched some TV (they had cable, we did not), and eventually, we all went to bed.

Five thirty AM.

Nothing good can come when there is a knock on your door at that time; but instead of being awakened by my mom, it was by my dad.

I admit to being a little groggy and confused; I could not understand at first the gravity of what my dad was saying, his afflictions made it difficult to understand him. After a few minutes, I realized he was telling me that he called 9-1-1 for my mother, and that the EMTs were in the bedroom with my mom as we spoke, working on her. I saw the EMTs and told them that I had her medical power of attorney, that she had a DNR and wanted no extreme measures taken.

My pragmatism then prevailed, so I was making a list in my head of what needed to be done before we went to the hospital, knowing that was beyond my father's capability at that point.

Let the dog out, feed her and change her water, brush my teeth, etc. The list was running through my head. Then I saw them wheel my mom out on the gurney and proceeded to get my dad in the car. We had a little tousle as to who would drive, but I told him I would take my own car if he insisted on driving; this had been an ongoing battle for a couple of years now. Today, I had no stomach for a fight: *I won.*

The ambulance got there before we did, and we were ushered into a private waiting room. The minutes ticked slowly by, and my dad and I were each wrapped in our own little worlds as we waited for news, any news. I called both my brother, Mark, and Aunt Dee Dee, my mom's sister, to let them know what was happening. I knew my brother would kill me when he next saw me for calling at this time in the morning, because I knew ultimately, everything would be fine; I just thought they should know that mom was at the hospital.

After about a half hour, the doctor came in to talk to us. I do not really know what he said, because I just picked up on the vibe that he was speaking a lot of words to hide the meaning of his news, and that the news was not optimistic.

They had been working on her, he said, and finally 'got her back', but were taking her to have a CT scan done to find out how much brain damage she may have experienced from the time she was down: longer than twenty minutes. He would let us know when he knew anything more.

I was stunned into incoherence. I was not sure what we should do; I thought about calling my brother and my aunt again, but it was still so early (funny how deep-seated social protocol is). I finally decided to go ahead and call them, knowing that I was overreacting to the situation and sure that we would all have a good laugh at my expense later. I do not believe my brain was ready to accept the news that I heard, and I was trying to internally negotiate any means of escape I could by that point. I know I heard that she was down for twenty minutes, but that was not making sense to me right now.

Aunt Dee Dee told me she was already getting ready to come, and I tried to tell her I should call her back with an update before she did that. She was, however, very insistent that she was coming – *now*.

My dad told me that he needed to use the restroom, so I was alone in the room when the nurse came in to let us know we could go see my mom. I told her I wanted to wait for my dad, but I asked what the prognosis was. She said something about her being intubated, and I was already aware of the CT scan, so I asked exactly how bad she was.

The nurse told me that when my mom came in, her pupils were fixed and dilated, and that she had never seen anybody come back from that.

Huh?

I questioned her further, knowing my mom's wishes and having her medical power of attorney. I asked if intubation and CT scans are usual and customary in this instance, and she responded that no, they were extreme measures. I conveyed that I had my mother's medical power of attorney and that, in fact, the hospital had it on file. I wanted to know, because I had told the EMTs the same thing; why had this happened?

She seemed surprised and told me that my father had told the EMTs to do 'everything medically available'.

I said, "Then we have a problem; this is everything she didn't want done. How can we un-do this?"

The nurse told me that, once intubated, the coroner was the only one who could remove the tube.

I asked the nurse to take me back to see her immediately.

As soon as I saw her, I knew she was gone. This was the shell that housed my mother, not my mom. A shell that was having a difficult time breathing. My dad came in at that time, and I asked, "What did you do? This is exactly everything that she did not want to happen."

He hung his head and said, "I wasn't ready to let her go; I was supposed to go first." I put my hand on his and said, "Dad, your plans and God's are not necessarily the same; we have to let her go."

Brokenhearted, looking small, and so very fragile, he said, "Yes, I know."

The nurse, who was still standing there, caught my assenting nod to stop life support. She told us that they would like us to leave the room so that they could 'do what was necessary'. We stood in the hall, my father losing his only stronghold to life, his life partner, his best friend; me losing my mother, my confidant, my strength, and my best friend.

And I was the one who had to tell them to do it.

As much as I wanted to uphold her wishes, I absolutely did NOT want to lose the one and only grasp to sanity that I had, because she 'got' me like no one else; this was the single hardest thing I have ever done in my life.

When the nurse came out and told us we could go back in, I noticed that the tubes had miraculously disappeared. I mouthed "Thank you" to her, and she tipped her head in acknowledgment, then left us to say our goodbyes.

Now it was a waiting game.

As hard as she struggled to catch every breath, we expected it to be rather quick. Every gasp she took felt like another dagger in my heart. So many thoughts were going through my mind, and when I was alone in the room with her, I apologized for not having been there for her, for not protecting her, for not stopping my dad from doing to her exactly what caused her to give me her medical power of attorney in the first place.

Even as I felt guilty for pulling life support, I knew that was what she would have wanted. We had had a discussion on what circumstances she would and would not tolerate, and at what point she wanted to go. I must say that her answers surprised me. Her distinction was quite more stringent than mine, as she even considered a pacemaker an 'extraordinary' measure, to which I said we would need to discuss that further later.

But there was no 'later', and in the end, I guess it did not really matter. My thought was that if she considered the pacemaker an extraordinary measure, pupils being fixed and dilated would be a simple parameter.

I excused myself to call Aunt Dee Dee and my brother to update them, now that things were making more sense to me, and to let them know there was no hope, that it was just a matter of time before life slipped from her. So much for my thoughts of 'overreacting' to her hospital visit; they had proven out.

So, we waited.

Aunt Dee Dee arrived at 9:00 or so, and my mom was still with us, gasping for breath and seemingly fighting for her life; I felt horrible.

By 10:00 AM, they told us that they were preparing a room for her, as we were still in the ER. So, we all moved up to room 221; a number etched in my memory for all time. And we waited some more.

By now, we knew she was holding on 'for something', but it was a guessing game as to what that was. We called Mark and had him talk to her and to say goodbye. Then we called Uncle Curt, her brother, explained the situation and had him say goodbye. We had each said our own goodbyes; and yet, she pressed on.

At 1:30 PM, I turned to my aunt and said, "She's waiting to hear from Savanna." She agreed but said she did not want to say anything about that. Since I had left intending to be in this situation with Aunt Mickey, and not my mom, I could not exactly call my daughter and say, "Hey, change of plans: say goodbye to Mema instead of Aunt Mickey."

I called my good friend, Doris, who also knew my daughter. I explained the situation and asked if she was available to be with her when I broke the news over the phone, as Savanna was particularly close to my mom. She said was available and told me she would await further instruction as to how to carry this out.

But even as she agreed, and I knew Savanna would be in good hands, in my heart it just did not sit well with me. Savanna had a special bond with my mom, and I knew I had to be with her in person to tell her. I just hoped that the three-hour trip to get to Savanna would not be too late for my mom's timeframe; I left immediately.

It was the longest three hours I have ever driven, because I knew at the end lay my daughter's broken heart; and I was the one who was going to break it.

When I got home, she was out, as I expected. I knew she had plans, but I did not know for sure with whom, or where they were. I texted her to ask where she was. She told me, and it was only a block from the house, so I asked her to come home. Remember, she was under the impression that I was three hours away and would not be home until tomorrow; this was her first clue that something was very wrong.

She called in response, and asked, "Is this the phone call I was expecting?" I told her no and asked again that she please just come home. She began crying, and said, "Oh, no: Baga!" The name she called my dad. I repeated, "Honey, just please come home, now."

She walked in the door with, I am sure, much trepidation. I asked her to sit on the couch with me and took hold of her hands. I started to explain how it was that her Mema was in the hospital, but at the first mention of 'Mema,' she began keening, and crying in a way I had never heard from her before, or since.

Her whole soul was in that cry, and I was right. Not only had her heart broken, but I knew her little world was in shatters; much as mine.

She calmed down a bit, and I was able to tell her that we needed for her to call and let Mema know that it was OK to go. She did not really understand the concept, so I told her about the whole day, and that she seemed to be waiting for 'something,' and that was the reason I was there: to ask her to call Mema and tell her it was OK, that she could let go.

It took about forty minutes for Savanna to calm down enough to speak to Mema. In the meantime, I worried that between the drive and the amount of time it took for her to get herself under control, the whole thing would be pointless; that I would have missed the chance to be with my mother at the hour of her death, and that Savanna still would have missed the chance to say goodbye.

As it turned out, she was able to speak her peace. Savanna had asked me what to say, and I told her that she would know what to say: to speak from her heart to Mema's. All that Mema needed to hear was her voice, and that she loved her; the details did not matter.

She took the phone and spent about ten minutes saying her goodbye. I left her alone for privacy and used that time to update Mark.

Savanna called me into the living room and asked to please go see Mema. I think we both knew that she would be gone by then, but it did not matter. So, we left. We got "the call" about an hour into the drive. She had passed at 7:07 PM.

With Mema's passing, I asked if Savanna wanted to continue, and she did; she needed to say goodbye in person.

The great thing about small towns is that they respect humanity more than large cities. One of the Deacons from my parents' church was there with our family, and 'knew somebody' at the hospital who was able to arrange to hold my mom's body there, in the hospital room, so that Savanna's last visit with her Mema would not be in the back room of a mortuary.

And they had cleaned her up very well. When we finally arrived, a little after 9:00 PM, she looked as though she was sleeping; we said our final goodbyes, and we took my father back home.

Each of us, in our own ways, alone.

Goodbye, Mema. We love you.

Savanna's Mema